Jazz

Jazz

A STUDENT'S AND TEACHER'S GUIDE

GRAHAM COLLIER

CAMBRIDGE UNIVERSITY PRESS

THE RESOURCES OF MUSIC SERIES
General Editors: *Wilfrid Mellers, John Paynter*

Published by the Syndics of the Cambridge University Press
Bentley House, 200 Euston Road, London NW1 2DB
American Branch: 32 East 57th Street, New York, N.Y. 10022

ISBNS: 0 521 20561 1 hard covers
       0 521 09887 4 paperback

First published 1975

Typeset by Keyspools Ltd, Golborne, Lancashire

Printed in Great Britain by Tinling (1973) Ltd, Prescot, Merseyside

Contents

Acknowledgements

My grateful thanks are due to Charles Fox for his invaluable help in lending records and reading over the manuscript in its various drafts, though I must take sole responsibility for all errors and over-generalisations.

I would also like to express my appreciation to William Shepherd of the Cambridge University Press who has been unfailingly helpful through all the traumas of deadlines etc. and has been of great assistance to me in fitting the writing of this manuscript into what has, luckily, become a very busy life.

I would also like to thank my musicians for their efforts on the accompanying album and tape. It was not always easy for them to think back to first principles, but they seemed to manage very well. The recording sessions also brought back to us – who are sometimes typed as avant garde players – that there is a great joy in playing a very simple 12-bar blues – and that it is not easy!

Thanks for permission to reproduce photographs are due to the following:

Richard Davies (jacket, paperback cover and frontispiece); Valerie Wilmer (pp. 17, 51, 71); Max Jones (p. 30); Quartet Books (p. 41); David Redfern (p. 60).

'It is the blend of the personal and the social, the aesthetic and the economic, that makes Jazz reflect our century so faithfully.'

Charles Fox,
Jazz in Perspective

Foreword

This book is designed to assist the teacher in covering jazz, either as part of the regular music curriculum or as a specialised course. It may be advisable though to discuss first what jazz is – or, perhaps more important, what it is not.

Jazz is not, as many people seem to think, synonymous with 'pop' – although it was once the popular music of the world.

It is not a raucous, collectively-improvised din played exclusively by Negroes in bars and brothels – although parts of the definition have fitted the music at various times.

It is not a pianist tinkling away on 'Pennies From Heaven' in a night club – although what he is playing may have some jazz elements.

All these misconceptions – and others too numerous to mention – have some truth in them but they are not, as their believers seem to think, the only answer. Jazz is a very small word but everybody seems to have their own strong views as to what it is – and whether a person 'likes it' or not is often based on a casual hearing of one small section of the music. This, not unexpectedly, leads to great confusion. One has only to pause and think of the chaos which would ensue if people were so indocrinated – and that is what has happened for reasons too complex to go into now – about any other art. 'Oh I hate modern poetry, I can't stand Ogden Nash' or 'I hate orchestral music, I can't stand Mantovani'. The juxtapositions are absurd, yet many people make similar misjudgements regarding jazz.

What then is jazz? Basically it is an improvised musical expression of a man's individuality. There are very often 'colourings' on this individuality – such as a steady pulse from the rhythm instruments and a wide variation in instrumental timbre drawn mainly from what are known as Afro-American sources – but these are not always necessary. Unsatisfactory though the definition may be, and even though overlapping with other musics, it is the only definition wide enough to cover the variety of musics classifiable as jazz. When one recalls that these range from traditional bands like Louis Armstrong's through big bands such as Duke Ellington's to avant garde groups such as Cecil Taylor's, one can see the extent of the problem.

It should also be realised that jazz should not be judged in comparison with 'straight music'; they both of course use the same basic language (as do poetry, prose and plays, but nobody tries to compare, on absolute terms, *Hamlet, Ulysses* and *The Four Quartets*), yet there still remains a faction that regards jazz as a poor relation because it does not possess the structural qualities of straight music. (The term 'straight music' will be used throughout the book to refer to all so-called 'classical', 'serious', 'orchestral', 'symphonic' etc., etc., music, because it is, to my mind, less inaccurate than the other terms.) Good jazz has something of its own to offer. As composer Bill Mathieu said when discussing the Gil Evans/Miles Davis collaborations, 'What is involved is the union of idea with emotion, pre-composition with improvisation, discipline with spontaneity' and that definition can be applied to all good jazz.

Paradoxically the greatest strength of jazz is the very aspect which makes it most difficult to appreciate. I refer to its *creativity*, the improvisation content which is essential to jazz and which, ideally, makes all jazz performances (even those by the same player) sound different. A devotee of any other art can be certain that, regardless of his subjective reaction to it, the art-object itself remains unaltered. Any number of performances of, say, Beethoven's Fifth Symphony will sound essentially the same, because the notes will be the same; any number of readings of *Ulysses* or *The Four Quartets* will not alter the words themselves. In jazz the object itself is constantly changing: each performance offers up, at the least, new variations on the given material and, at the most, a completely new structure. Familiarity with a performer's style is an advantage but one can make no preconceived quality judgements about the content. Each performance is, as Lawrence Durrell said, 'a new adventure, a raid on the inarticulate' and must be approached as such. Recordings of jazz performances give the illusion of permanence but, in almost all cases, recordings are simply one *performance*, a frozen moment of time, and care should be taken that they are not unthinkingly regarded as the *definitive* performance of a particular piece or the *ne plus ultra* of the player's style. Jazz is an art without any of the built-in safety-nets of status or familiarity. All that is left, unsatisfactory as it may be to a teacher, is a subjective reaction to a personal statement from the musician.

Concern is often expressed over the apparent limitations of a 'repetitive' pulse or 'restricting' chord patterns and, though there have been considerable changes since the late 1950s, it should be remembered that it is the *superimpositions* of other rhythms – other chords over the basic pulse and chord patterns – that make jazz interesting. Yehudi Menuhin, when recording with a jazz rhythm section, was moved to remark that the basic pulse was 'like pillars around which the soloist can dance'. Similarly jazz players are not confined to the basic chords either horizontally (when passing notes, both chromatic and non-chromatic, are used) or vertically (when substitutions, alterations and additions, and passing chords are common): again it is the superimposition that is important and here rhythmic complexity often combines with harmonic complexity as the chords are 'placed' in the time continuum.

Linked with these apparent restrictions are two real ones: a dependence on theme – solos – theme as a basic form in many jazz performances; and a lack of development, meaning a general lack of connection, written or improvised, between the parts of that form. There have been various attempts to break away from these restrictions but there is the constant tension between too much control on the one hand (which restricts the soloist) and too much freedom (which may lead to chaos) on the other. But, again, one must not fall into the habit of comparison with straight music. As critic Don Heckman pointed out in *Downbeat* magazine's 1964 annual, 'Instead of building musical ideas upon pre-determined forms like the sonata, jazzmen tend to think of form as a verb – to construct their music as they go along.'

There is no doubt that jazz today is a minority art: it has had an influence on twentieth-century popular music and continues to do so in contemporary rock groups; it brought back improvisation into the main stream of western music, and it has had a considerable effect on instrumental techniques; but it still remains a mystery to many and a noise to some. There is no chance that it will return to being *the* popular music (freak Top Twenty hits do appear, but then so do hit versions of Mozart and Richard Strauss), and the temptation must be resisted to equate it with pop – even though one perhaps may see similarities of feeling between the Top Twenty and some jazz. The temptation must also be resisted to compare it with straight music – and again one may perhaps see similarities between the two (particularly in the avant garde). Jazz must be treated as a separate entity: as a music in its own right capable of moving people to tears or ecstasy – or a music capable of banality. This book points out various things about jazz musicians and jazz music, both from a 'music appreciation' and a practical point of view, but it can only suggest things to listen to, things to try, things to study further. The rest is up to the student and ultimately all that is left – and it is of immense importance – will be his personal statement as a player and his personal reaction as a listener.

The author

Graham Collier was born in 1937 in Tynemouth, England. After spending seven years (three of them in Hong Kong) in a British army military band he won a scholarship from *Downbeat* magazine to the Berklee School of Music in Boston. While there he studied with Herb Pomeroy and recorded two tracks ('The Barley Mow' and Billy Strayhorn's 'Star Crossed Lovers') for the school's *Jazz in the Classroom* series. The latter track prompted the comment from Bill Mathieu while reviewing the record in *Downbeat* that 'Jazz is not being written better than this.' During 1963 Collier toured with the 'ghost band' of Jimmy Dorsey, but left after a bad car accident and returned to England.

The first edition of Graham Collier Music – a 'west coast' sounding septet was formed in 1964 and fast established a favourable reputation. The first recording was made in 1966 and there have been five subsequent albums. In 1967 he became the first jazz composer to receive a bursary from the Arts Council of Great Britain and he used the award to start an exploration on which he is still engaged. This stems from the belief that jazz composition should, as far as possible, express the essential characteristics of jazz improvising; its ability to be fresh at each performance. The Arts Council commission became known as *Workpoints* and the approach has been further developed in *Mosaics* and *Songs For My Father*.

He has also written many more conventional band pieces and he has often fulfilled commissions for festivals etc. His music is often heard in other countries, either on band tours, through writing assignments for bands abroad or by transmission of recordings. He has also written music for documentary films, television commercials and a stage play.

His interest in education started with visits with the band to schools and his own teaching assignments at the various jazz schools in Britain. His own band has been called a nursery for fledgling jazz talent and has included at various times Karl Jenkins and John

Marshall (later with The Soft Machine), Stan Sulzmann (later with John Dankworth) as well as Richard Pearce, Frank Ricotti, Alan Wakeman, Geoff Castle and John Webb. He has written two other books on jazz, is single and lives in London.

REFERENCES

PUBLICATIONS

Inside Jazz (Quartet, 1973). A guide to jazz for the layman.
Compositional Devices, based on Songs for My Father (Berklee Publications, 1974). A package of text, scores and record.

RECORDS

Deep Dark Blue Centre (Deram, 1966)
Down Another Road (Fontana, 1969)
Songs For My Father (Fontana, 1970)
Mosaics (Philips, 1971)
Portraits (Saydisc, 1973). Available with scores.
Darius (1974). Available with scores.
'The Barley Mow' on *Jazz in the Classroom*, Volume VII (Berklee, 1962)
'The Star Crossed Lovers' on *Jazz in the Classroom*, Volume VIII (Berklee, 1963). Composed by Billy Strayhorn, arranged Graham Collier.
'Gay Talk' on *The National Youth Jazz Orchestra plays . . .* (Philips, 1973)

MAJOR WORKS

Alexandria Quartet (1966); *Deep Dark Blue Centre* (1966); *Burblings For Bob* (1967); *Workpoints* (1968); *Contrapuntal Forms* (1968); *Suite Sandy Brown* (1969); *Songs For My Father* (1969); *Smoke Blackened Walls and Curlews* (1970); *Where will they Put the Blue Plaque Now?* (1970); *And Now For Something Completely Different* (1971); *Wheel of Dreams* (1972); *Children of Adam* (1972); *Facets* (1973); *Sea, Sky and Down* (1973); *Rosemary for Remembrance* (1973); *An Odyssey (some thoughts on Space and Time)* (1973/4); *Darius* (1974).

Introductory notes

The book is divided into two sections: the first covers the history and sociology of jazz through the lives of various individuals; the second deals with the practical aspects of playing jazz.

The seven individuals discussed in Part One (Louis Armstrong, Duke Ellington, Django Reinhardt, Charlie Parker, Miles Davis, Dave Brubeck and Ornette Coleman) were chosen in order to present the history of the music in terms of individual people, rather than the more usual chronological approach with its almost inevitable listings of little-known names and inaccessible recordings. In these essays are considerations of a variety of other aspects of jazz, both musical and sociological, and it is hoped that these will provide connections between jazz and music generally and also with society.

Each chapter is self-sufficient. Within each chapter, three or four reference lists for further information are given, including:

1. Listening: recordings mentioned or recommended recordings of artists mentioned.
2. Further reading: references to other books or sections of books.
3. Projects: some suggestions for work and discussion on matters raised in the text and on related subjects, both inside and outside music.

Each chapter concludes with

1. Points to listen for
2. Suggested records (with dates of 'best period')
3. Further reading.

Part Two deals with the practical side and begins with a discussion of the problems involved in teaching jazz. There are eight subsequent chapters (Improvisation; The blues; The popular song form; Arranging; The big band; Modes and scales; Jazz composition, and Contemporary trends). Each consists of an essay followed by practical material. Again references are given for listening and further reading.

The third section is a series of appendices to supplement the musical theory.

Finally, the Glossary will explain the terms which might be unfamiliar in the text. The only notation which should be explained in advance is the use of m or — for minor chords.

One of the problems of the beginning jazz player is that, unless he is extremely lucky, he will not have a rhythm section of piano, bass and drums available to him, and though some adjustments can be made, for much jazz playing this is a necessity. There is also the problem that even if they are available they may be at the same standard as (or possibly worse than) the student himself. Bearing this in mind Geoff Castle, John Webb and I have recorded some piano, bass and drums accompaniment tracks for common jazz situations. These include various blues, with both simple and complex chords in a variety of time signatures; two common 32-bar progressions; two common modes, and a contemporary chord sequence. These are available on a tape.

A record of illustrations of some of the practical points raised in Part Two is also available. These are all detailed as they occur in the text. The use of these by the student as a comparison with his own efforts and as an indication of what can be achieved will, I'm sure, prove invaluable.

As a general introduction to jazz, I have also recorded a version of the lecture concerts which I have been presenting in schools for many years. This deals with the history and musical content of the music and is complete with a booklet expanding some of the points raised and giving many references for further listening and reading.

Of the references quoted in the book, unfortunately but inevitably some will be out of date by the time it is published. This applies particularly to recordings, which are issued, deleted and repackaged with bewildering speed. Record libraries or specialist jazz shops (who advertise in the jazz magazines) may be able to supply the actual record mentioned or be able to offer a sensible alternative. Beware though of inexpert advice; an indifferent recording of a jazz artist (and almost all have made such recordings) will just be a waste of money and time. Great care must be taken, and specialist advice sought, over choosing recordings. (Records such as *The Essential . . .* or *The Indispensable . . .* are often good but they are only one record company's output, and an artist may have been with several different companies in his career.)

The recently issued *Jazz Anthology – from King Oliver to Ornette Coleman* (CBS), a moderately priced 4-record set is an ideal companion to the text and availability is promised for several years. It will be referred to often and noted in the references as *Anthology* after the specific track. Apart from the tracks referred to in the text, it includes representative pieces by many other prominent musicians. It is particularly strong on pianists, including Earl Hines, Art Tatum, Errol Garner, Fats Waller, Meade Lux Lewis, Ahmad Jamal and Bud Powell.

The following books are strongly recommended as general introductions: Gunther Schuller's *Early Jazz* (Oxford, 1968), Charles Fox's *Jazz in Perspective* (BBC Publications), dealing succinctly and interestingly with the chronological history of jazz. My own *Inside Jazz* (Quartet Books, 1973, also available in a paperbound edition), a non-technical guide to jazz for the layman, which explains in simple terms much that is taken for granted in this book (such as familiarity with instruments, general styles of jazz etc.) and would therefore be a good starting book for school children. André Hodier's *Jazz, its Evolution and Essence* (Secker & Warburg, 1956).

REFERENCES

RECORDINGS

Published by Cambridge University Press and available from booksellers, record shops or direct from the publisher:

Collier, *Jazz Rhythm Section*   Tape
Collier, *Jazz Rhythm Section*   Cassette
Collier, *Jazz Illustrations*   LP
Collier, *Jazz Lecture Concert*   LP and booklet

PART ONE

1 Louis Armstrong

The early history of jazz

It is fitting that Louis Armstrong, who in so many ways typifies jazz to much of the world, should, in his own career and influences, reflect the musical and geographical developments of its early stages. He was born, appropriately enough, on American Independence Day, 4 July 1900, in New Orleans – a city generally held to be the birthplace of jazz, and at a time when the various strands that went to make up jazz were gathering together.

New Orleans was a flourishing sea port, which had become the home of many former slaves. Armstrong's own great grandparents and grandmother were slaves from the Gold Coast of Africa (now Ghana) and the music such slaves brought into America, particularly the call and response patterns of their work songs, was strongly influential in the development of jazz. Another influence was the music of the settlers, mainly French and English, in particular the melodies and strong basic pulse of their marches and the harmonic base of their hymns. This blending of musics (which was also happening in other parts of the southern states, but to a lesser degree) first developed into spirituals (Negro songs of worship) and blues, and then into the music which we now know as jazz.

The music of the church was also a strong influence on Louis Armstrong. He said, 'All that music that's got a beat, it comes from the same place, from the old sanctified church', and this influence can still be seen in much of jazz. The early music in the Negro churches was Protestant hymns – forced on the slaves by their 'Christian' masters – but this was soon added to and developed into a music much more exciting than we are used to hearing in church. It has a great joy and spontaneity about it. The congregation participate in the service with tambourines and handclapping and often join in the service with exclamations like 'Oh yea, my Lord' at appropriate moments. A skilled preacher plays on this, developing a 'conversation' with the congregation by singing or saying a phrase which the congregation

answer – thus continuing the call and response tradition of the work songs, a tradition which later came back into jazz with its use by the big bands of the swing era.

Another place of music in New Orleans was the streets. The Negroes had learnt European instruments (though they played them with a more personal 'vocalised' tone) and European march tunes, and these were heard – altered by some decoration of the melody – in street parades to celebrate almost anything. They were also heard in funeral processions, and such funerals, reserved for anyone of importance in the area, were often accompanied by several bands. The music on the way to the burial was slow and sad, often hymn tunes like 'Nearer My God to Thee'. On the return though, once they were a respectable distance from the cemetery, the band would break into a brighter time with faster marches like 'Oh Didn't He Ramble'.

Louis Armstrong, as a boy, used to follow these parades and later played in them. He also heard ragtime music (a highly syncopated and formalised piano style – again a strong formative influence on jazz) and blues sung by itinerant guitar players. Originally a sad song the blues became formalised into a 12-bar, three-strain structure, not necessarily sad. The aura of the blues – the musical inflections and personal message – permeates Armstrong's playing, and in fact all true jazz.

Armstrong's first chance to play an instrument came in the waifs' home (where he had been sent at the age of twelve for celebrating New Year's Eve by firing his stepfather's gun in the street) and here he graduated to cornet after playing, briefly, many other instruments. At first he was only a part-time musician like most in New Orleans, and he made a living at one time by selling coal. His playing engagements were often in the taverns of the Storyville district – often known as the 'Tenderloin' or simply 'The District'.

This area – which had sprung up to cater for the needs of the men on the ships using the port – had music in all its bars and brothels. The brothels were known as 'sporting houses' and used solo piano players ('professors') to provide the musical entertainment. The most famous of these was Jelly Roll Morton, self-styled 'inventor of jazz' and, without question, the first real jazz composer. He was fifteen years older than Armstrong and one of the most colourful characters in jazz, invariably flashily dressed and wearing a $\frac{1}{2}$ carat diamond in his teeth. He had little regard for Armstrong, considering Freddie Keppard to be the better player. Morton, like Keppard, was a creole (of mixed blood, from African and Spanish or French stock) and creoles looked down upon the American Negroes, considering themselves to be of a much higher position in life.

The bands that played in the bars were commonly six men strong – cornet, clarinet, trombone, banjo or piano, bass and drums. The music they played was quite often in the 12-bar blues form and many titles (still played today) immortalised streets in the Storyville district such as Basin Street and Canal Street. It was collectively improvised with each of the instruments having its own clearly defined role making up melodies and countermelodies around the main theme. The cornet (sometimes replaced by a trumpet) played the melody, not as originally written but with variations around it. The clarinet created an upper countermelody (derived traditionally from the piccolo counter-melodies of the marching bands). The trombone decorated the harmony – often sliding between notes (glissando) – and provided a lower countermelody. The drums and bass (usually in those days a brass bass – either a tuba or sousaphone) provided the basic pulse, strongly derived from the marching band tradition. Piano and banjo or guitar gave the harmonic basis.

Pure solo playing, apart from 'breaks', was rarely heard in such music, and listening to early recordings today one is struck by the repetition of material and lack of space. It must be remembered though that objective judgement about early jazz on the strength of recorded examples is almost impossible. Recording techniques were crude and many generally acknowledged great musicians – including the legendary Buddy Bolden – rarely recorded. Many early Negro musicians *refused* to record in the fear that their ideas would be stolen from them and in fact the first jazz group to record was a white band – the Original Dixieland Jazz Band in 1916. The fact that their jazz was reportedly inferior to that of contemporary Negro musicians (and much more popular) was the first of a distressingly long series of examples of white musicians exploiting the superficialities of jazz while more creative Negro musicians starved. (This is not said to make a racialist point but to stress the fact – discussed in more detail later – that jazz was born a Negro art and, though most of the major contributors to the music have been black, the major successes in commercial terms have been white.)

Though at first found primarily in New Orleans, jazz and its associated musics, such as ragtime and blues, began to spread around America aided by the itinerant blues singers and the entertainment on the river boats which travelled the major waterways of the southern states – particularly the Mississippi and Missouri. Such boats used many bands from New Orleans and it was here that Armstrong learnt to read music.

Many musicians left the river boats at one of the more northern ports of call and moved on to Chicago, but the main exodus of jazz from New Orleans came with the closing down of Storyville in 1917 (for its effect on the morals of the US Navy). This was linked with the mass migration of the rural Negro population of the south to the industrial cities of the north and the migrants' need for their own kinds of entertainment.

Armstrong moved to Chicago in 1922 to join his idol Joe 'King' Oliver, a very highly rated cornet player from New Orleans – hence his title. Oliver's playing was eventually overshadowed by Armstrong and he died in obscurity in 1938 but his band in Chicago was highly thought of and represented what Gunther Schuller called in *Early Jazz* 'the last ditch stand of the New Orleans style'. It was, like other New Orleans bands, polyphonically based but with four collectively improvised voices (two cornets, clarinet and trombone) in place of the traditional three. It was Armstrong who helped make the band so successful in Chicago, and it was Armstrong who, some years later, made it outdated by the strength of his soloing. Armstrong changed jazz from a collectively improvised music to one where the individual soloist is predominant – a concept which has remained largely unaltered to this day.

REFERENCES

LISTENING

Work songs – *Negro Prison Songs* (Tradition).
Negro church music – *The Gospel Sound* (CBS).
Funeral and marching bands – *Eureka Brass Band* (Atlantic).
Ragtime – *Scott Joplin Ragtime* (Biograph).
Original Dixieland Jazz Band – *Livery Stable Blues* (RCA).
New Orleans style – 'Gate Mouth', *Anthology*.
King Oliver – 'Snake Rag' (1923), *Anthology*.

FURTHER READING

On African influence – *Early Jazz*, chapter 1.
Savannah Syncopators by Paul Oliver (Studio Vista, 1970).
Jazz in Perspective, pp. 12–19.

On religious music – Chapter 2, 'Duke Ellington', and references in that
    section.
On blues – Chapter 10, 'The blues'.
    Jazz in Perspective, pp. 14–18.
On Jelly Roll Morton and life in New Orleans around 1900 – *Mr Jelly Roll* by
    Alan Lomax (Cassell & Co., 1952). Subtitled *The Fortunes of Jelly Roll
    Morton, New Orleans Creole and Inventor of Jazz*.
On New Orleans – *Jazz in Perspective*, pp. 21–9.
On race – Chapter 3, 'Django Reinhardt'.
On King Oliver – *Early Jazz*, pp. 77–86.

PROJECTS

On New Orleans as a city – Geographically, historically and musically. Duke
    Ellington recorded a *New Orleans Suite* (Atlantic, 1970).
On slavery.
On the development of western straight music and jazz.

His influence

In 1924 Armstrong went to New York, again paralleling a move jazz
itself was making around that time, to join the big band of Fletcher
Henderson. It was in Henderson's band that Armstrong started to
shine. His solos were far superior to those of the other musicians on
the band – even Coleman Hawkins who later, after being strongly
influenced by Armstrong, became almost entirely responsible for the
development of the tenor saxophone in jazz. Armstrong's solos were
exuberant and seemed to dance over the generally pedestrian rhythms,
while the other soloists stayed very close to the pulse and the basic
chord tunes. Louis even then showed a sense of space and an ability to
build a solo architecturally by the development of his ideas, while the
other soloists tried to crowd their ideas, giving their solos no room to
breathe (still a fault with many jazz soloists).

  Armstrong's melodic concept – both then and later – influenced
composing and arranging, in that he showed new ways of interpreting
melody and of filling in between melodic statements. His rhythmic
approach – the way he placed his notes in relation to the steady pulse
of the bass and drums – had a lot to do with the developments leading
to the 'swing era' (the period in the middle and late thirties when big
bands such as Benny Goodman and Count Basie gained great popularity with a style which juxtaposed simple repetitive figures – known
as 'riffs' – over a strong pulse).

Between 1925 and 1928, in Chicago, Armstrong made a series of recordings under the name of Louis Armstrong's Hot Five and Hot Seven and it was these recordings that began to show the real possibilities of jazz, moving it away from being purely an entertainment music played on the streets and in bars and dance halls to being an art; still entertaining as all art should be but, as Gunther Schuller said, 'This was music for music's sake, not for the first time in jazz, to be sure, but never before in such a brilliant and unequivocal form.' Armstrong also showed that jazz could express the emotions and personality of an individual, and that in the process valid music could be instantly created. He laid the foundations for jazz as we know it – the improvised solo statement on previously presented material. He also showed new tonal possibilities for the trumpet and indeed for all jazz instruments by incorporating all manner of vibratos, glissandos, growls, shakes and gradations of tone into his technique. Many of these devices are apparent in his singing and illustrate the influence of the vocal traditions in jazz and the desire of the jazz musician to express *himself* through his instrument: to make his style of playing as personal as his handwriting or voice.

Armstrong extended the range of the instrument considerably as well as increasing its tonal possibilities, but his main contribution was the *content* of his solos. Simply put, it is the choice of notes and where he places them that makes Armstrong into a major soloist. Like all good players he knows the value of tension and release both in aspects of rhythm and pitch; he will, for example, often hit a high note and hold it for a considerable time before releasing the tension with some descending, short note, phrases. As has been mentioned he knows the value of space, of not crowding his ideas nor trying to get too many notes into a phrase. Each chorus sounds inevitable and right yet retains elements of the unexpected. Armstrong's influence can still be seen in contemporary trumpet players and Miles Davis has said, 'You know you can't play anything that Louis hasn't played – I mean even modern.'

His most acclaimed recording of this period was 'West End Blues' which includes a brilliant final chorus commenced by a high B♭ held for 4 bars, a charming duet between Johnny Dodds' clarinet and Armstrong's scat singing ('nonsense' syllables in the style of an instrumental improvisation) and a declamatory, almost fanfare-like solo cadenza to begin the piece. Of this Schuller says, in *Early Jazz*, 'These two phrases alone almost summarize Louis' entire style and his contribution to jazz language. The first phrase startles us with the powerful thrust and punch of its first four notes. We are immediately aware of their terrific swing, despite the fact that these four notes occur on the beat, that is are not syncopated, and no rhythmic frame of reference is set. These four notes should be heard by all people who do not understand the difference between jazz and other music, or those who question the uniqueness of the element of swing. These notes as played by Louis Armstrong – not as they appear in notation – are as instructive a lesson in what constitutes swing as jazz has to offer. The way Louis attacks each note, the quality and exact duration of each pitch, the manner in which he releases the note, and the subsequent split second silence before the next note – in other words the entire acoustical pattern – present in capsule form all the essential characteristics of jazz inflexion.'

REFERENCES

LISTENING

Fletcher Henderson – 'Sugarfoot Stomp' (1925), *Anthology*. Discussed in *Early Jazz*, pp. 275–7.
  'A Study in Frustration' (3 records, CBS).
Hot Five and Hot Seven ('West End Blues', 'Wild Man Blues', 'Potato Head Blues', 'Beau Koo Jack', 'Hotter than That' are particularly good.) – 'West End Blues' (1928), *Anthology*. Discussed in *Early Jazz*, pp. 115–19.
  The Best of Louis Armstrong (Parlophone).
The *Anthology* also includes Armstrong on 'St Louis Blues', sung by Bessie Smith, accompanied by harmonium, and 'Weather Bird', a duet with Earl Hines on piano. Discussed in *Early Jazz*, pp. 124–6.

FURTHER READING

On big bands – *Early Jazz*, chapter 6.
On Fletcher Henderson – *Early Jazz*, chapter 3, pp. 90–5.
On Hot Five (1926) – *Jazz, its Evolution and Essence*, chapter IV.
On Hot Five and Hot Seven – *Early Jazz*, chapter 3, pp. 98–130. Includes transcriptions of solos.

The problems of popularity

Records such as *West End Blues* were great commercial successes and Armstrong's reputation was established by the late twenties – at least in the Negro ghettoes and, strangely enough, in Europe. White

American audiences did not get much chance to hear Armstrong either live or on record at that time as jazz records were largely confined to jukeboxes in predominantly Negro areas such as Harlem, and concerts and tours rarely played for white audiences. Europe though had avidly taken to jazz through recordings and tours – such as those Armstrong made in 1932 and 1933.

His reception was generally ecstatic – though some people did walk out of his London concerts calling it 'hell music'. However, on his second visit, the weekly music paper *Melody Maker* levelled an accusation of deliberate commercialism at him saying that his concerts were '50% showmanship, 50% instrumental cleverness, 0% music'. Such charges were increasingly made against him and he was often accused of exploiting racial characteristics of the Negroes for entertainment purposes (known as 'Uncle Tom' behaviour after the character in *Uncle Tom's Cabin*).

But such criticisms are unfair. Armstrong was *always* an entertainer in the widest sense of the word – even his most influential solos were designed within an entertainment situation (records or public appearances) and were never meant to be regarded as 'art' or 'culture'. The fact that these solos were influential and, as Schuller says, 'established the general stylistic direction of jazz for several decades to come', was by the way. Armstrong existed in a world where he worked to make a living and the so-called 'Uncle Tom' characteristics were simply part of the entertainment language of his early days. He did not consciously work to change the direction of jazz or to make himself famous, but having done both before he was thirty it is perhaps understandable that he did slacken off and live off his past successes. It must be remembered though that all his work – even his vocals on standard material – is strongly jazz-influenced and is unique. For Armstrong in all his music fully illustrates the jazz tradition of individuality – the expression of a player's personality through his approach to sound and through his interpretation of melody – and his was the first major expression of such individuality in jazz.

From the late 1940s, Armstrong toured the world extensively with a small band known as The Louis Armstrong All Stars, concentrating less on playing (he was after all around fifty by then) and more on singing. He was immensely successful and many of his records (songs like 'Mack The Knife', 'What a Wonderful World' and 'Hello, Dolly') achieved hit parade status. He had of course always sung and his early work strongly influenced the development of popular singing. He was one of the first singers to apply jazz phrasing and the concept of jazz improvising to the usually banal material of the hit parade. Each interpretation was new; some notes were lengthened, others shortened; the pitch of some notes was altered by deliberate flattening or sharpening, then sliding into the correct pitch; vibrato was used to colour some notes; the whole contour of the melody was often altered. It was the application of such devices by Armstrong that strongly influenced Bing Crosby and Frank Şinatra and, through them, all contemporary popular singers.

It does seem ironic though, and indeed says a lot about the position of jazz in today's society, that the man who had so much influence on the development of jazz should be best known for his clowning and for his versions of tawdry songs like 'Hello, Dolly'. There would seem to be no parallel here with other arts – mainly because in other arts there is not the dichotomy between entertainment and art that has grown up in jazz since 'West End Blues'.

In its beginnings jazz was purely an entertainment music played in clubs and dance halls, or a practical music played for funeral and other processions. With the flowering of Armstrong in the late 1920s came what could be called 'art as entertainment' – music played primarily 'to amuse' but possessing enough musical content to reward repeated listenings. With the new explorations that came to fruition in the 1940s and became known as 'bop', little conscious attempt was made to entertain as such (though of course the music was entertaining to many people), and 'art for art's sake' came into jazz. Musicians like Charlie Parker expressed dislike at having to play in night clubs and being treated like mere entertainers rather than artists. These three streams co-exist in jazz today: the pure entertainment of many dixieland bands; the art as entertainment of, say, Duke Ellington; and the art for art's sake of much of the avant garde. Such co-existence is the cause of many problems in people's appreciation of jazz – a word which is held to have a narrow meaning dependent on the listener's likes and dislikes, rather than a wide meaning embracing many different kinds of music.

Armstrong's success and genius were such that he appealed to people across the jazz spectrum from fellow musicians ecstatic about such performances as 'West End Blues' to a general public who accepted 'Hello, Dolly' as a unique statement from a warm human being – and accepted it without being aware that Armstrong was only displaying a tiny proportion of his talent.

Music like 'West End Blues' will never get to the hit parade – as Schoenberg said, 'If it is art it is not for all; if it is for all it is not art' – but we must be thankful that Armstrong was able to produce such work and, perhaps, regretful that the pressures of commercialism forced him into more mundane fields. There is no denying though that he was the first genius in jazz and it is a mark of the esteem with which he was held by his contemporaries that when recording 'Louis and His Friends' – about a year before he died (6 July 1971) – that in the choir for a version of the John Lennon tune, 'Give Peace A Chance', were such widely different jazz musicians as Eddie Condon, Miles Davis and Ornette Coleman, paying tribute.

REFERENCES

LISTENING

'Hello, Dolly' (Coral).
'Louis and His Friends' (Phillips).
Louis Armstrong All Stars – *Satchmo at Symphony Hall* (Coral).

PROJECT

On entertainment and art – 'Armstrong changed the course of jazz while merely entertaining'; discuss the concepts of entertainment and art. Is all art entertainment? Is all entertainment art?

GENERAL

POINTS TO LISTEN FOR

1. his warmth
2. the way he interprets the given melody
3. his tonal resources (both on trumpet and in his singing)
4. the way he builds a solo (development of ideas)
5. his sense of space (not crowding ideas)
6. his use of tension and release (pitch and rhythm)
7. his use of the full range of the trumpet
8. his 'swing' (the way he places notes against the basic pulse).

SUGGESTED RECORDS (best period 1928–32)

The Genius of Louis Armstrong (CBS). Two albums of very good tracks of 1924–32 including 'West End Blues', 'Wild Man Blues', 'Potato Head Blues' and 'Beau Koo Jack'.

The Best of Louis Armstrong (Parlophone). Contains Hot Five and Hot Seven
recordings, and early big bands.

FURTHER READING

Louis, The Louis Armstrong Story by Max Jones and John Chilton (Studio
Vista, 1971). A well documented biography, informally written, if
somewhat rambling. Well illustrated.
Satchmo, My Life in New Orleans by Armstrong (Davies, 1955).

2 Duke Ellington

The problem of the big band

Duke Ellington's position in jazz history is comparable to that of Louis Armstrong. Improvising existed before Louis' Hot Five and Hot Seven recordings but it was these recordings which showed how exciting and personal a statement jazz improvising could be. Similarly composition existed in jazz before Ellington but it was he who first showed that it was possible to write jazz in such a way that the musicians were free enough to express themselves while the piece stayed unmistakeably the composer's. In other words, Ellington discovered a way of solving the basic dilemma in jazz: if it becomes organised the musician's freedom is inhibited; if it is left unorganised then chaos may result.

Ellington's aim was always to retain the flavour of small group jazz – its intimacy and its freedoms – in the context of a larger group. (Such groups in jazz are rarely more than sixteen musicians.) He achieved this by writing for the individuals of his band. He knew the qualities of each musician both on his instrument and personally – even, as he said once, 'how they play poker'. This is of course in direct contrast to a straight composer who normally writes, as it were, in abstract and whose work can be played by any group of similar size and will come out sounding almost exactly the same. Ellington's compositions are peculiar to his band; another band could play the manuscript but the sound would be different because other individuals would be involved. As Billy Strayhorn, who worked with Ellington for many years, said, 'Each member of his band is to him a distinctive tone colour and set of emotions, which he mixes with others equally distinctive to produce a third thing which I like to call the Ellington effect.'

Duke Ellington treated his written scores as 'points of departure'. He would reshape them drastically in rehearsal and would often add new sections on the spot. These could be based on the recollections of a phrase that one of the soloists improvised at a recent performance,

and this would be added to until it became an integral part of the tune –
or in some cases the basis for a complete composition. His orchestration
was also often changed on the spot as he realised that, as Strayhorn
said, 'The man and the part weren't the same character.'

There is a constant change of textures in Ellington's writing. Unlike
conventional big band writers who voice from the top down regardless

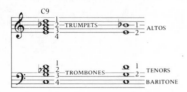

Ellington would change the order depending on the quality he
wanted – in other words voicing people rather than instruments.
Similarly he would often have the melody *inside* the harmonies and
bring it out by careful balancing of the voices.

The harmonies also have an individual texture because of this
concern for individual sounds. The baritone sax (played by Harry
Carney who was with Ellington from 1926) is often used very high to
give a certain 'buzz' to the harmonies, and Ellington would utilise
this to add colour notes to chord-dissonances which veil the chord and
make it individual, interesting and often difficult to analyse properly.

He also writes 'across the band', rarely dealing in saxes alone or
brass alone but choosing combinations of instruments from all that is
available. When dealing with voicings like the following (and you
must remember that the full flavour can only be brought out by the
Ellington band)

it is easy to appreciate the story, attributed to André Previn, that 'Stan Kenton can stand in front of 20 musicians make a grandiose gesture and every composer knows what the chord is. Duke Ellington stands in front of three musicians, flicks his little finger, and nobody knows.'

Edward Kennedy Ellington was born in Washington in 1899 (the 'Duke' came later – not as a title bestowed on him in England, but rather as a tribute to his suave elegance). He started his playing career as a pianist and bandleader for society dances but his first influence was the 'stride' piano style (a very full, almost orchestral, way of playing developed from ragtime). His early compositions reflected this influence as well as the debt he owed to his early musicians, in particular trumpeter 'Bubber' Miley and trombonist 'Tricky Sam' Nanton. As their names begin to imply these two players created an enormous variety of sounds from their instruments which they utilised in their solos and in the compositions they worked on with Ellington.

At that time Ellington's style was still being formed. He chose musicians for their uniqueness and was in turn heavily influenced by them. Each piece the band performed explored some new aspect of composition or orchestration as Ellington learnt by trial and error which devices worked and which did not. Much of this experimentation was done during the band's tenure at the Cotton Club (a night club run by gangsters in Harlem, the Negro district of New York). Many of the show pieces that were put on for the white socialites slumming it in Harlem could perhaps be called racialist in today's terms, in that they were pseudo-jungle production numbers dealing with the heritage of the Negro race; but it was providing the music for such items that led Ellington – and his musicians – to explore the possibilities of jazz instruments much deeper than they would perhaps otherwise have done. Listening to the Cotton Club recordings today one hears many interesting ideas hinted at which were later explored more fully. One can also hear how, even for a mundane production number – like 'Arabian Lover' or 'Haunted Nights' – Ellington produces effective music, but music which has a tongue in cheek wit also.

By the thirties Ellington had become very popular. Many of his songs had become hits and melodies of that period, such as 'Mood Indigo', 'Solitude' and 'In A Sentimental Mood', which have retained their popularity till today. He was also constantly improving his craft, and the records he made between 1938 and 1942 show him and the band at their peak.

A comparison of Ellington's work with any of the other big bands of the period shows how much more musical he was. His slower arrangements were texturally far beyond anything else that was going on (though, of course, many of the subtleties of the orchestration were lost on the listeners) while his faster numbers equalled the swing and excitement of bands like Benny Goodman's, and the soloists were often better. Each piece had a wealth of interest in the composition and orchestration that other bands lacked.

By this time Ellington had mastered the problem of writing within a 3 minute form (the average length of a single record – long players having not yet been invented). Even a straightforward blues composition had a continuity of ideas as opposed to being merely a string of solo choruses. Each piece seemed to possess the same qualities:

- a good basic melody
- plenty of freedom for the soloist
- interesting textures (both instrumentally and harmonically)
- some melodic development (by means of paraphrase or written out 'improvisationary' passages)
- some interest in the form such as interludes, modulations, new material, etc.

Each piece seemed inevitable (which should not be confused with predictable) and perfect. There was no sense of rush yet the soloists had time to express themselves and the compositions stayed unmistakably Ellington's.

Confusingly though, Ellington by this time was using another writer, Billy Strayhorn – composer of such beautiful tunes as 'Lush Life' and 'Chelsea Bridge' (inspired not by the bridge itself but by Whistler's painting). Strayhorn also wrote 'Take the A Train', the band's signature tune and perhaps the best known composition attributed to Ellington. This confusion in the public's mind is very understandable. The two men worked extremely closely together and it is almost impossible to tell who wrote what in a specific composition.

In the band from 1940 to 1942 was Jimmy Blanton, a young bassist whose way of playing the bass altered the rhythmic approach of the Ellington band and transformed the instrument's role from 4 beats in a bar to a more melodic line. Blanton heralded the improvisatory approach of present day bass players such as Charles Mingus, Richard Davis and Ron Carter.

Also making important contributions to the band were Harry Carney, the baritone sax player mentioned earlier; Johnny Hodges, an alto sax player with a felicitous habit of slurring between notes and a passionately lyrical ballad style; trombonist Lawrence Brown – another lyrical melodist like Hodges; and Ben Webster. Webster's broad breathy tone added a new dimension to the orchestral palette and a superb solo voice to the already impressive roster of improvisers. He was strongly influenced by Coleman Hawkins but his style is a curious mixture: sensuous and breathy on tunes like 'Chelsea Bridge'; gutsy and attacking on 'Cottontail' and 'Just a Setting and a Rockin''.

These musicians and the others in the band helped Ellington to create his sound and enhanced it with their solos, which by present-day terms are short and may seem restricted but, as composer William Russo pointed out in a *Downbeat* magazine review of an Ellington record of this period, the soloists in Ellington's band, by subordinating themselves to the whole, have 'ironically achieved so much more originality than they might have if they had proceeded along more standard lines'.

REFERENCES

LISTENING

Stride piano style – 'Carolina Shout' (James P. Johnson), *Anthology*.
Cotton Club period – *Cotton Club Days* (Ace of Hearts).
   Any titles like 'Haunted Nights', 'Jungle Nights in Harlem' will give some idea of the period.
1927–40 Covered extensively on *The Ellington Era*, Volumes I and II (3 records in each volume, CBS).
   'Black and Tan Fantasy', *Anthology*.
1938–45 *The Indispensable Duke Ellington* (RCA) includes 'Chelsea Bridge', 'Mood Indigo', 'Black and Tan Fantasy' and two duets with Jimmy Blanton.
   In a Mellotone (RCA) includes 'Just a Setting and a Rockin'' – a brilliant example of call and response, and 'Cotton Tail'.
   At His Very Best (RCA) includes 'Concerto For Cootie' and 'Harlem Air Shaft' (a picture of what can be heard down a Harlem air shaft).
Jimmy Blanton – 'Blues', *Anthology*.
Johnny Hodges – 'All of Me' (1959), *Anthology*.

FURTHER READING

Early Ellington style – *Early Jazz*, chapter 7. Includes Cotton Club period and musical examples. Reported to be first part of two-part study by Schuller of Ellington.
The big bands – Chapter 13, 'The big band'.
On 'Concerto for Cootie' – *Jazz, its Evolution and Essence*, chapter VI.

PROJECTS

On a comparison between Ellington and other swing era bands.
On Russo's point of achieving originality through subordination.
On pictorial music – Taking Strayhorn's 'Chelsea Bridge' – or any pictorial piece – as a basis, explore programme music generally, narrowing down perhaps to a discussion on whether jazz which calls on improvisation is capable of depicting such scenes. Ellington always said he had a picture in mind in his descriptive pieces. These could be played 'blindfold' to students asking them to give their impressions as a written project, in painting or even mime or dance.
On co-operative art – Following on from the point about the way Ellington, in common with most jazz composers, worked with a specific band, influencing them and being influenced by them, compare this with ballet, theatre and straight music. How much credit should the leader take for the co-operative effort?

His achievements

Duke Ellington, either alone or in collaboration with Billy Strayhorn, wrote several long compositions. Quite often though they are – as in *Black, Brown and Beige* and his recent *Far East Suite* – simply a collection of shorter pieces with little or no thematic connection. He seems to be essentially a miniaturist, satisfied and satisfying in the 3–4 minute form. His attempts at more complex forms rarely hang together and are unsuccessful as extended compositions, though of course parts of them are still good. In his religious piece, 'In The Beginning God', for example, the initial 6-note motif, though well conceived as an expression of the hope and majesty inherent in those four opening words to the Bible, was very much over-used in the composition. (That motif incidentally was conceived in almost exactly the same way by Ellington and Strayhorn working completely independently of each other. They thought of the same starting and concluding note and had only two notes different in the complete six.)

Ellington was always known as a religious man and we are told that he read the Bible daily. His 'Come Sunday' from *Black, Brown and Beige* is surely one of the loveliest melodies in jazz. He said of 'In The Beginning God' that it was his way of worship, countering criticism by saying 'every man prays in his own language and there is no language that God does not understand'.

Ellington also performed his versions of other people's music – both pop and classical. Most surprisingly he reworked the music of *Mary Poppins* (a Julie Andrews film of the mid-sixties) and recorded an album of songs by the Beatles. He also wrote, with Billy Strayhorn, versions of Grieg's *Peer Gynt Suite* and Tchaikovsky's *Nutcracker Suite*. The latter is the more successful of the two, being an almost complete reworking of the suite in the Ellington band's own terms. 'Dance of the Sugar Plum Fairy' (renamed 'Sugar Rum Cherry') is made into a very sensuous melody – a duet between Harry Carney (baritone sax) and Paul Gonsalves (tenor sax) – and is much earthier than Tchaikovsky ever imagined it.

Ellington long showed an interest in the stage – stemming perhaps from his Cotton Club days – and wrote many musicals, including *My People* which was performed in Chicago. He never, however, wrote for the Broadway stage, though he did say that as soon as he could get someone to put it on he would sit down and write it out. But he wrote the music for several films, including *Anatomy of a Murder* and *Paris Blues*, and for productions of T. S. Eliot's *Murder in The Cathedral* and Shakespeare's *Timon of Athens*. This latter led him to write – again in collaboration with Strayhorn – a Shakespearean suite called *Such Sweet Thunder*. Described modestly enough by Ellington as 'his attempt to parallel the vignettes of some of the Shakespearean characters in miniature sometimes to the point of caricature', it is in the main successful. 'Star Crossed Lovers' for example – with Juliet depicted by Johnny Hodges' alto and Romeo by Paul Gonsalves' tenor is a sadly beautiful melody which could be said to emulate the unfortunate pair.

Interestingly the four so-called sonnets, ('Sonnet for Caesar', 'Sonnet to Hank Cinq', 'Sonnet in Search of a Moor' and 'Sonnet for Sister Kate') all use the 14-line sonnet form as their musical base. (John Dankworth later used two of these melodies for settings of actual Shakespeare sonnets for singer Cleo Laine: 'After some delving into 154 suggestions by William Shakespeare, Cleo and I hit upon two which seemed to fit the respective tunes, albeit in very different ways.')

One point of regret is that Ellington was till the end unsuccessful –

and, sad to report, often embarrassingly so – in his attempts to write for large groups of strings. The reasons behind this failure – and he is by no means alone – are gone into in more detail later, but it would seem that he was unable to get to grips with the *individuality* of the players: they were anonymous men and Ellington only wrote well if he knew their personal idiosyncracies – 'how they play poker'.

If Ellington failed to write an extended composition that is wholly successful, and failed to write for a string section effectively, it is regrettable, but of no great importance when measured against his achievements. He towers above all other composers and arrangers in jazz in his ability to blend successfully composition and improvisation. He solves the paradox implicit in the term 'jazz composition' more often and more entertainingly than any other jazz writer. Every writer who attempts to write jazz has been influenced by him – and most show it quite obviously. One can see the direct influence in such writers as Gil Evans, Charles Mingus, Mike Gibbs and Carla Bley (and in my own writing). None of these writers deliberately attempts to copy Ellington but none can avoid the influence. They may use different approaches to harmony and have different concepts of rhythm and melody, but they are still trying to solve the same problem: to be themselves while leaving enough freedom for the musicians to be themselves; in other words to be a true jazz composer – a role which Ellington may not have invented, but one which he fitted to perfection.

REFERENCES

LISTENING

Black, Brown and Beige (includes 'Come Sunday'). *At His Very Best* (RCA).
'In The Beginning God', *Concert of Sacred Music* (RCA). Also includes two
    versions of 'Come Sunday'.
Other religious music in jazz – *Second Sacred Concert* – Ellington (RCA).
    Light In The Wilderness – Dave Brubeck (MCA).
    A Love Supreme – John Coltrane.
    And the gospel inspired music of Charles Mingus, 'Better Get It In Your
        Soul' and 'Wednesday Night Prayer Meeting' on *The Art of Charles
        Mingus* (Atlantic).
Mary Poppins (CBS).
Beatles songs (CBS).
Peer Gynt (CBS).

Nutcracker (CBS).
Far East Suite (RCA).
Such Sweet Thunder (CBS).
Cleo Laine's versions – *Shakespeare and All That Jazz* (Fontana). Includes
    settings of two Ellington sonnets and other Shakespeare material by
    Dankworth and Arthur Young. Great singing.
Ellington and strings – *The Symphonic Ellington* (Reprise). Works best on
    slower piece but writing is often bad, sometimes embarrassingly so. 'La
    Scala She too pretty to be blue' has some 'purple' passages reminiscent of
    Hollywood movie scores at their worst. (In fairness I must point out that
    critic Leonard Feather rates it highly.)

COMPOSERS SHOWING THE ELLINGTON INFLUENCE

Charles Mingus – 'Gunslinging Bird', *Anthology.*
    Charles Mingus (Prestige).
Gil Evans – See Chapter 5, 'Miles Davis'.
Carla Bley – *Escalator Over the Hill* (JCOA). Records a fascinating mix of
    contemporary musics including rock, avant garde, etc. Features many
    jazz stars.
Mike Gibbs – 'Just Ahead' (2 albums, live recording, Polydor).
Graham Collier – See pp. xi–xii.

FURTHER READING

On jazz composition – Chapter 15, 'Jazz composition'.

PROJECTS

On religious music – A discussion of Ellington's point about every man pray-
    ing in his own language; of religious music generally and in jazz.
On comparison of versions – of Beatles songs, *Peer Gynt, Nutcracker,*
    Shakespeare sonnets (including other versions).
What's in a name? – Is an evocative title sufficient to convince us that a non-
    specific piece has a specific connotation? Does 'Star Crossed Lovers'
    effectively portray Romeo and Juliet? Does it matter that it was origin-
    ally a song (with words) written by Strayhorn and called 'Pretty Girl'?

The problems of age

The fact that Duke Ellington lived till his seventies and was still a
creative artist till he died may not in itself be so surprising – we are
accustomed to artists in all fields who work long past what is called
retiring age. Picasso, Stravinsky, Pablo Casals . . . all seemed destined

to go on creating for ever and still produced good work in their eighties and nineties. The reason for this is that creativity is a renewing process. As Polly Toynbee pointed out in her book *A Working Life*, 'The mind is like a stomach: it expands or contracts to suit the requirements.' She said that after working all day on a boring job, all she wanted to do was slump down in front of the television set; but after a day as a journalist her mind felt alive: ready for new adventures, new ideas.

That creative artists continue working into old age is then understandable, but when one considers the comparative isolation from the world of an artist like Picasso, compared with the gruelling schedule of concerts around the world undertaken by Ellington, one realises how remarkable it is that he still continued composing. That he survived till he did in a profession as vulnerable as jazz (when many musicians have been forced to leave by the pressures involved, been killed in road accidents or succumbed to addiction) and in an art as demanding as jazz (where one is expected to create anew at each performance) is surprising – and somewhat miraculous.

A further point is that jazz has always been considered a young man's music: Jimmy Blanton, who revolutionised the bass and rhythm sections generally, died in his early twenties of TB, as did guitarist Charlie Christian, responsible for many of the changes in jazz which led to bop in the 1940s: Charlie Parker, who expanded on Christian's (and others') ideas and changed the language of jazz died at the age of 34: Louis Armstrong recorded his revolutionary solo on *West End Blues* when he was 28 and Miles Davis made important contributions with 'Birth of the Cool' when he was 23 and 'Kind of Blue' when he was 32.

It would seem then that the major developments in jazz have been made by people in their twenties or early thirties. What happens then? Once a jazz musician has made a major step forward or found his own style how does he continue to develop?

Most of course do not. Many drop out for financial reasons or because the pressures of such creativity are so great. Others take to drugs or drink to try to combat such problems and either die or lead a wasted life. Those who survive do so in a number of ways between that chosen by Louis Armstrong (a deliberate commercialisation of his talent which, though it brought many new people into jazz who might otherwise not have heard it, was regrettable) and that chosen by Miles Davis (a constant renewal of his creativity by exploring new directions – in Miles' case by the orchestration of bop in 1949; the use of modes in 1958; the use of electronics and rock rhythms in 1967. Ellington himself lay somewhere between the two, in that he pioneered a style of composition and jazz orchestration and achieved his great period when he was around forty years old. From then he was, like Armstrong, wildly successful on an international basis. Like Armstrong too he has often been accused of commercialisation and of 'selling-out' in that his programmes often contained old, fairly shallow material, but as Billy Strayhorn has pointed out there is a great problem with a man of Ellington's popularity and vast output, that he *had* to play requests (though Miles Davis would simply say 'listen to the records'). It does seem a pity, however, that, with such an immense amount of almost unheard material available, Ellington should have devoted time at his concerts to selections of old tunes, and not-too-good vocalists.

Along with this repetition of old material and pandering to popularity Ellington did write many new compositions and he showed that he was still capable of creating new works and developing within them the style he himself created.

It is possible that this accent on youth in jazz developments so far in its history may alter as jazz moves away from the nightclubs and dance halls and into the concert halls. Whether it does remains to be seen – we are after all only in the seventies of the history of jazz itself. Certainly successful jazz artists now have more respect and can reap higher financial rewards from records and composition royalties than they have done before and this may lead to a slower pace than was allowed to a man like Armstrong – or indeed Ellington. As to Ellington's continuing creativity while he was constantly travelling and performing, the truth for him lay in Billy Strayhorn's comment 'You have to be out there in the world. Otherwise you can't feel the heat and the blood. And from that comes music, comes feeling.'

REFERENCES

PROJECTS

On the stimulation of work – Based on Polly Toynbee's quote (from *A Working Life*, Peacock).

GENERAL

POINTS TO LISTEN FOR

1. use of call and response with band and soloist or two soloists
2. moving inner lines
3. paraphrase of melodies and complete reworking of melodies
4. descriptive tunes ('Chelsea Bridge', 'Harlem Air Shaft')
5. freedom for the soloist
6. interesting textures (instrumentally and harmonically)
7. development of form.

SUGGESTED RECORDS (best period 1939–42)

(NB Later records should be heard in stereo as the lines and textures will be
   reproduced better.)
In a Mellotone (RCA).
At His Very Best (RCA). Both of the best period.
And His Mother Called Him Bill (RCA). The band's tribute – played with love –
   to Billy Strayhorn, who died in 1967.

FURTHER READING

Music is My Mistress (W. H. Allen, 1974, Quartet paperback, 1975). A fascinating autobiography, including many personal – but few musical – in-
   sights.
The World of Duke Ellington by Stanley Dance (Macmillan, 1971). Includes
   articles by Ellington and many of his musicians.

3 Django Reinhardt

Is jazz only a Negro art?

Many people in jazz – musicians, critics and fans – believe that jazz is unquestionably a Negro music. Its roots were in Africa, its flowering came in the southern states of America amongst the Negro descendants of African slaves, and all major developments in jazz have come from Negroes. The extreme holders of this view say that white musicians have stolen the Negro styles and made money while the originators starved; the more moderate viewpoint is that some white musicians can play jazz but you have to be a Negro to play it properly.

The latter viewpoint is perhaps equivalent to saying that as we originated cricket in England, only English people can play it and that everyone else is stealing our ideas. The fact is that England *has* been beaten by teams from the West Indies and India. The game is now universal and although English players may still be very good they are not *necessarily* the best in the world. Though there is a stronger case to be made for Negro predominance in jazz than that for English predominance in cricket, it is no longer possible to say that only Negroes can play jazz, or even that they are necessarily the best jazz players in the world.

Initially, if this predominance of Negroes in jazz were to be challenged – especially in the 1920s and 1930s when jazz was becoming established both musically and socially – one would have expected the challenge to come from white Americans. They would be nearer the source and would possibly have played with Negro musicians. There are in fact two white musicians of that era who are generally acknowledged to be extremely good jazz players: Bix Beiderbecke (who played with Paul Whiteman) and trombonist Jack Teagarden (who was later with the Louis Armstrong All Stars for many years). One would not however have expected such a challenge to come from outside America. Recordings of jazz were still fairly limited (though often more popular in Europe) and chances to hear jazz musicians live were rare, but a Belgian born guitarist of that period, Django Rein-

Django Reinhardt

hardt, had a great influence on jazz guitar styles and one can still find excitement in his improvisations today.

Django Reinhardt (in both names the 'd' is silent) was a *manouche* (a French-speaking gypsy) born in Belgium in 1910. He spent much of his early life travelling around France and Belgium in his mother's caravan (he was in fact twenty before he lived in a house). His first exposure to music was, naturally enough, the traditional gypsy music, most often semi-improvised and played on stringed instruments like the guitar, mandolin and violin. He started to play guitar at the age of twelve, teaching himself by watching and imitating others and showing remarkable precocious talent. He first played professionally at the age of thirteen when he played banjo in a dance hall, a *bal-musette*, and as Charles Delauney says in his book on Reinhardt they were 'the meeting places of thieves, spivs and prostitutes' – not so different from the brothels and bars of Louis Armstrong's early days in New Orleans. At eighteen he was offered a contract to appear with Jack Hylton, the famous English bandleader of the time, but a caravan fire, in which he was severely burnt, prevented this and indeed almost ended his life.

With remarkable determination Django recovered from his injuries – which included the loss of two fingers of his left hand – and learnt to play the guitar again. His first exposure to American jazz came soon after when he heard recordings of Ellington, Armstrong and violinist Joe Venuti, and this influence alongside the semi-improvisatory style he had already developed gave him a life-long devotion to the music, and made him into a remarkable exponent of it.

His dexterity on the guitar is astounding, even when one disregards his handicap and the developments on the instrument since. The runs he played still sound exciting – and difficult in technical terms – and the chord voicings and improvised fills he used still sound fresh. His tone was warm and very human and his whole playing style reflects his gypsy heritage with its curious mixture of flamboyance and delicacy.

Perhaps the best examples of his talent are shown on the recordings he made for the original Quintet of the Hot Club of France, a group formed under the auspices of one of the many small societies in Europe designed to encourage the growth of jazz. This group had the usual instrumentation of violin (played by Stephan Grappelli – a conservatory trained musician), three guitars (a soloist – Django – and two rhythm players, including Reinhardt's brother Joseph) and a string bass. The absence of drums was compensated for by the steady 'chunky' beat of the rhythm guitars and because of this, and the two soloists, the group achieved a marvellous exuberant swing unique in jazz and one never recaptured even by subsequent versions of the Quintet. The material they played was, in the main, popular songs of the times, such as 'Rose Room' and 'Lady Be Good'. Reinhardt himself, though reluctant to admit it, could not read or write music (or indeed write at all; he had laboriously to learn to sign his name for contracts, etc.), but he composed many beautiful melodies – written down by his friends – such as 'Manoir de mes Rêves' and 'Nuages'. Not surprisingly he possessed a remarkable musical ear and aural memory and some of the 'Improvisations' he recorded at that time are structurally perfect.

He played the acoustic (non-amplified) guitar almost exclusively, an instrument which since the arrival of the easier-to-play amplified instrument has been sadly dropped from jazz. (He did try the electric instrument in 1950 but failed to sound convincing on it.)

As an individual Reinhardt was exasperating to his friends and musical colleagues. Like many gypsies he felt somewhat superior to ordinary people (who were regarded as 'peasants') and often acted in a very arrogant way. He sometimes failed to turn up for jobs and occasionally returned to the road with his relations. He took his status as a star seriously and often made unrealistic demands regarding fees and presentation. He was once only dissuaded from making a grand entry by being lowered into his place on wires by a sudden remembrance of his superstitious fear of heights! He had many arguments with his musicians regarding money and he often cheated them.

Reinhardt's fame had spread around the world through recordings and when, in Occupied France in 1943, he was arrested on suspicion of spying he was soon released by the commandant who was a fan of his music! Most of his life however was spent playing in France with French musicians, but he did record in Paris with visiting Americans such as Coleman Hawkins and Benny Carter. His plans to visit America were prevented by the war but he did tour there in 1946 with Duke Ellington (accompanied only by Ellington at the piano, not the entire band) and plans were laid for him to tour with Norman Granz's *Jazz At The Philharmonic* but these were prevented by his death in 1953 of a stroke.

In his last years, Reinhardt played little and he was often called 'old-fashioned' as the new developments of bop (which had been heralded by another guitarist, Charlie Christian, and brought to fruition by Charlie Parker and Dizzy Gillespie) took hold of musicians and fans. A reassessment of his music today may show old-fashioned rhythm section concepts, ideal however for the Quintet at that time, but his own technique and improvising talent still sound fresh and exciting. Without doubt he was the first non-American jazz musician worthy to be called 'great'.

REFERENCES

LISTENING

Bix Beiderbecke – 'Singin' the Blues', *Anthology*.
Jack Teagarden – 'Moonglow', *Anthology*. With Louis Armstrong All Stars.
Hot Club of France recordings – Best with Stephan Grappelli, the original group.
'Manoir de mes Rêves', 'Nuages', 'Improvisation'.
   Complete listing available on *Djangologie* (19 volumes, EMI).
   Representative tracks on *Django Reinhardt and Stephan Grappelli and the Hot Club of France* (Ace of Hearts) and *Parisian Swing* (Ace of Hearts).

FURTHER READING

On the African heritage – *Early Jazz*, chapter 1.

PROJECTS

On folk musics – Hungarian (ref. Bartok); Spanish; African and jazz; commercial folk.
On guitar styles – Classical; Flamenco; folk; pop and rock jazz. Amplified and acoustic. Comparison of sounds.
On gypsies.

Towards a wider definition of jazz

Django Reinhardt's standing amongst jazz musicians is best illustrated by the fact that one of the best compositions in jazz was written in homage to him when he died. This is John Lewis's 'Django'. It was originally written for and recorded by The Modern Jazz Quartet but it has since become a jazz standard and has been recorded by such as Stan Kenton, Gil Evans and Miles Davis. It is a simple, very moving melody with overtones of Django's gypsy heritage. After the almost processional opening, the tempo changes for the improvisations – which are based on a different chord sequence from the opening though one derived from it. There are allusions here to the New Orleans funerals with the slow march to the cemetery followed by a happier return.

How is it then that such a man with no background in jazz and who only visited America once should be considered to be one of the world's great jazz musicians and have inspired one of jazz's best compositions? The answer lies in a consideration of Reinhardt's gypsy background in the light of a broader view of jazz than is generally contemplated.

Jazz cannot be regarded as purely an American Negro music – otherwise one must discount the playing of Bix Beiderbecke and Jack Teagarden and more recently the influence of pianist Bill Evans and composer/arranger Gil Evans. It is not even essentially an American music any more – one cannot ignore for example players like Dave Holland and John McLaughlin, both British, both members of recent Miles Davis groups. Jazz is not a matter of nationality, it is simply players improvising – usually over a rhythmic pulse and using more personal sounds than we are used to hearing in an orchestra, for example; essentially they are just expressing themselves through music (a further discussion of this is given in the Foreword and in Chapter 9, Improvisation).

This definition of jazz though is one that can be applied to other folk-based (as opposed to art-based) musics. Indian music for example has these elements, as does African music, and I would argue for a consideration of jazz wide enough to encompass the Indian musicians such as Ravi Shankar and the master drummers of Ghana alongside Miles Davis.

Looked at in this light the significance of Reinhardt's heritage becomes apparent. Gypsy music is semi-improvisatory (there is an aural tradition of passing down melodies which are considerably embellished in performance). Individual musicians and dancers can display stunning virtuosity in this way and become – as Django did – celebrities in their mainly self-entertaining communities. There is a parallel here in the self-entertainment tradition of the slaves from Africa and the status afforded to talented entertainers both inside and outside the Negro community. Because of its improvisatory nature and use of mainly stringed instruments the use of inflexions (bent notes, glissandi, etc.) is common in gypsy music – as in jazz. There is also a possible link between the Hindu origins of the Romanies (gypsies), the largely improvised Indian music and Gunther Schuller's theory of the blue originating in India and travelling, via Arabia, North Africa and Spain to the Caribbean and America.

Reinhardt's gypsy background, allied with his interest in jazz, established him as an important non-American jazz musician before the Second World War. It has taken longer for musicians without such a strong folk heritage to develop into original jazz players but increasingly more and more jazz musicians with original things to say are coming from Europe, and indeed other parts of the world. John Lewis said in the early sixties that 'a growing number of jazz musicians in Europe are developing fresh individual contributions to the language', and it may be that 'language' is the key word. It is learnt by listening and talking with others, and though an accent is almost always detectable it does not affect your communication in the language and there is nothing to stop you making an original contribution in art or science in that language. (The Russian novelist Vladimir Nabakov is a good example.)

Jazz musicians in Europe have learnt the language (by listening to records and by listening to and playing with visiting Americans) and can now converse on equal terms with jazz musicians both white and black. There has yet to be a major development by a European, equivalent, for example, to the modal experiments of Miles Davis, or the strong influence white American pianist Bill Evans had on his coloured contemporaries. Neither are there signs of a European jazz genius to join the select group of Louis Armstrong, Duke Ellington and Charlie Parker (people who have radically affected the music) but the possibilities of such a figure emerging are not to be discounted.

REFERENCES

LISTENING

Django (MJQ, original recording).

EUROPEAN ARTISTS

George Chisholm – British trombone player renowned for his humour and talent. The only European comparable to Reinhardt in the pre-war period.
Along the Chisholm Trail (77 Records).

Sandy Brown – British clarinet player with unique sound.
  Sandy Brown, with the Brian Lemon Trio (77 Records).
John Surman – British poll-topping baritone sax player, with remarkable extensions of range.
  The Trio (Dawn).
Albert Mangelsdorff – German trombonist.
  Live in Tokyo (ENJA).
Jean Luc Ponty – French violinist. Recorded and played with Frank Zappa and his Mothers of Invention.
  King Kong (Pacific).
John McLaughlin – British guitarist who played with Miles Davis, and has a track named after him on *Bitches Brew*. His own group, the Mahavishnu Orchestra, is world famous.
  Inner Mounting Flame (CBS).

FURTHER READING

On jazz composition – Chapter 15, 'Jazz composition'.
On British jazz – *Music Outside* by Ian Carr (Latimer Press).
  My own *Inside Jazz* (Quartet) has an account of some of the problems faced by jazz musicians in this country.

PROJECTS

Comparison of versions of 'Django', and other tunes common in jazz. For a list of possible points of comparison see the References to Chapter 12, 'Arranging'.
Discussion of a wider definition of jazz (following on perhaps from the earlier discussion on folk music).
Study of European or British jazz. Does it compare favourably with the jazz of the American Negro – or even American white musicians?

Racial problems

One must accept then that jazz is an international music with its innovating talent being generally American Negro but useful contributions coming from other races. Historically and proportionately, though, Negroes do predominate. In terms of success and financial reward however white musicians have predominated – at times at the expense of the Negro.

The most extreme example of this was the enormous popularity of Benny Goodman in the swing era using the style (and even the exact arrangements) of Fletcher Henderson, whose own band, though musically in advance of Goodman's, never achieved that same success. Henderson himself, though Goodman did in fact employ him for some time as pianist and arranger, died in comparative obscurity.

The 'hits' in jazz, tunes like Stan Getz's 'Desifinado' or Dave Brubeck's 'Take Five', have almost always been by white musicians, and white groups have always been more acceptable to audiences and promoters. When one considers such facts alongside the *general* prejudice in America against Negroes one can understand the frustration – and indeed anger – of many black musicians. Many coloured musicians left America and went to live in Europe where there is a more relaxed atmosphere for Negroes and where jazz has a higher standing than in its native country – there is almost certainly a connection here. The great soprano player Sydney Bechet lived for many years in France and even had a square named after him in Antibes. Ben Webster, the ex-Ellington saxophonist, lived in Europe for the last ten years of his life – mostly in Copenhagen or Amsterdam – and found the ambience there more acceptable than in America.

Others reacted in different ways. Louis Armstrong once had to announce his own radio programme when the regular announcer walked off saying 'I haven't the heart to announce that nigger on the radio' but, except for one well publicised blast about the integration issue at Little Rock in 1957 he was fairly quiet about racial problems. He was accused of being an 'Uncle Tom' and was not highly regarded by militant young Negroes. Duke Ellington, once told by a policeman that if he were white he would have been a good musician, performed many pieces about integration but rarely spoke about it.

In their defence though it should be remembered that both Armstrong and Ellington regard themselves primarily as entertainers and consider it wrong to mix politics with music. Charlie Parker however, was called the first angry black man. He once deliberately smashed the glasses his band had been drinking from in a white club so as not to 'contaminate the customers'. Since then jazz – which has moved from being primarily an entertainment to being primarily an art – has often contained political comment and the musicians have become more involved in problems of race. Composer Charles Mingus for example wrote 'Fables of Faubus' with highly derogatory lyrics about the Governor of Arkansas at the time of the Little Rock integration issue.

Among the avant garde black musicians there was a strong move to break away completely from the associations of the word jazz. They called their music 'Black Music'. Saxophone player Archie Shepp recorded a passionate tribute to the assassinated Negro leader Malcolm X in his poem 'Malcolm' and was in the forefront of this move. Shepp though still uses white trombonist Roswell Rudd in his bands and such inconsistencies are common.

It does seem by now, though, that jazz is strong enough and free enough for a Negro to write an elegy for an assassinated black power leader and for a British musician to use it, as I did, to portray the contrasts of the West Riding of Yorkshire. Both should be judged on the results – whether they are satisfactory individual statements – and the race of the composer or the musicians is immaterial. As Charlie Parker said, 'Music is your own experience, your thoughts, your wisdom. If you don't live it, it won't come out of your horn.'

REFERENCES

LISTENING

Benny Goodman – 'King Porter Stomp' (Fletcher Henderson), *Anthology*.
'Fables of Faubus' (Charles Mingus) on *Mingus Presents Mingus* (CBS).
'Malcolm' (Archie Shepp) on *Fire Music* (Impulse).
'Smoke Blackened Walls and Curlews' (Collier). A portrait of the West Riding of Yorkshire. Unrecorded at this time but still in repertoire.

FURTHER READING

On Black Music – *Black Music* by Leroi Jones (MacGibbon & Kee, 1969).

PROJECTS

On race.

GENERAL

POINTS TO LISTEN FOR

1. his instrumental technique (particularly his fast runs and chordal playing)
2. the melodic content of his solos and the sheer warmth and joy in his playing
3. his backings to other soloists (his use of rapidly articulated chords; his melodic lines and his use of repeated patterns)
4. the sounds he produced from his guitar.

SUGGESTED RECORDS (best period 1934–9)

Any of the *original* Hot Club of France recordings, i.e. those with Grappelli. Specially recommended tracks are 'Rose Room', 'Runnin' Wild', 'Liebestraum no. 3' (Liszt), 'Mystery Pacific', 'Improvisation' (solo), 'Nuages' and 'Manoir de mes Rêves' (the 1943 version is best with two clarinets and no violin), and 'You're Driving Me Crazy'.

FURTHER READING

Django Reinhardt by Charles Delauney, translated by Michael James (Cassell, 1961). Interesting account of Reinhardt's life and career. Includes complete listing of his recordings (557 single sides are listed).

4 Charlie Parker

The nature of the jazz musician's art

The nature of the jazz musician's art differs from that of almost every other creative person. Most creative artists work in isolation. The painter, the sculptor, the novelist, the composer, all work alone and, apart from pressures accepted by themselves such as deadlines or other commitments, work at their own pace. The jazz musician has to create at a moment outside his own control, a fate shared by actors, ballet dancers and orchestral players, though their job is usually more interpretive than creative.

Also, any creative art is competitive. The artist is forced to compete with others indirectly for jobs and critical acclaim and directly in a usually unspoken desire to 'come out best' with his contemporaries. Even a completely self-effacing artist who neither looks for work nor cares about his contemporaries is involved in competition with himself, constantly striving to improve his art. For the solitary artist this competition is controllable in that he regulates his own output and any work he dislikes can be scrapped. For the jazz musician such competition is rarely avoidable. He cannot cancel engagements because he feels that he will play below standard. He must pray that inspiration will come, but if it does not there is no way out apart, that is, from relying solely on his accumulated knowledge and technique and turning in a purely craftsman's performance instead of that of a creative artist. One off-night if recorded or badly reviewed can set back a musician's career considerably. The jazz musician has to keep playing; keep feeding what Whitney Balliett called 'the insatiable furnace of his improvisation'.

Also, whereas a painter or a novelist can still be creative into his sixties and beyond, and expect a possible career of forty or more years, jazz musicians often burn themselves out or die in their thirties or forties after a creative career of less than twenty years.

In jazz there is no financial security – though this is general to all the arts. Illness and family problems may take their toll of whatever

Charlie Parker

income there is and there is no guarantee that any temporary financial success will be continued – and of course there is no pension apart from that of the state.

These are creative pressures on the jazz musician which are not usually apparent in other arts. There are also pressures brought on by the kinds of environment in which jazz musicians, at least until recent years, have most often worked. There are the abstract pressures created by the fact that a jazz musician, who may consider himself an *artist*, has to work in night clubs to an audience who are, quite often, out merely to be *entertained*. Conversation, bar noises, waiters moving around are all distracting and affect the musician's sensibilities over a period of time. There is also the fact that a jazz musician often becomes elated by the performance and, especially in a strange town, has nowhere to go to continue his elation or 'come down' slowly.

Then there are the more specific pressures of the jazz environment – the late hours, the 'cash-in-hand' method of payment and the ready availability of drink, and very often drugs. It is not surprising therefore that with all these pressures jazz history is full of stories of musicians becoming alcoholics or becoming addicted to heroin and many lives have been tragically ended because of such problems. Not all jazz musicians have tried hard drugs or drink too much and some indeed are completely teetotal and against all stimulants. Of those who have been addicted to drugs, some have successfully conquered it. Miles Davis for example was hooked on heroin for several years but finally grew tired of his dependence on the drug and kicked the habit 'cold-turkey' (by sudden and complete withdrawal). Others though played well *while* addicted and it is not surprising perhaps that younger musicians, thinking that an injection of heroin would make *them* play well also, tried to emulate these addicts. Unfortunately it does not work out that way. As Charlie Parker said, 'Any musician who says he is playing better either on tea [marijuana], the needle, or when he is juiced, is a plain straight liar. When I get too much to drink I can't even finger well let alone play any decent ideas. And in the days when I was on the stuff [heroin] I may have *thought* I was playing better but listening to some of those records now I know I wasn't.'

That perhaps should be engraved on every jazz musician's heart – and should certainly have been engraved on Parker's own for he first tried heroin at 15, became addicted at 25, and died at the age of 35, looking as the coroner estimated 'around 53'.

REFERENCES

FURTHER READING

On heroin addiction – *Second Ending* by Evan Hunter (Transworld). A novel on addiction.

PROJECTS

What is creativity? – Can everyone be creative in some way or only the 'artist'?

Interpretation v. creativity – Is Yehudi Menuhin a lesser artist than Miles Davis because he interprets while Davis creates?

On addiction – Not only drugs, drink etc., but anything else – work, sex, television, bingo, music, etc.

The new directions of bop

Charlie Parker was born in 1920 in Kansas City (the birthplace also of Ben Webster, another great jazz saxophonist). At that time Kansas City was the commercial and entertainment centre for a large area of the United States, and gangster-run nightclubs proliferated. Jazz was a very large part of Kansas City life and as Ross Russell said in his biography of Parker, *Bird Lives*, 'Just as surely as Mozart grew out of the musical culture of 18th Century Salzburg . . . Charlie Parker was the product of another similarly intense and pervasive musical culture.' All the great jazz bands of the time played in Kansas City whilst on tour and all night 'cutting contests' (where musicians competed to see who was the best player) were common. Parker heard most of the major saxophone players in jazz while he was still in his teens – often by slipping out of his house at night and not returning till dawn.

Parker's seemingly effortless control of his instrument was gained through a tremendous application of work. He was largely self-taught and extremely enquiring. At once time he was laughed off the stage at an after hours session for the mistakes he made while trying to play a double-tempo passage while improvising on 'Body and Soul', but he persevered until he had it under control. He also practised the blues chord sequence in every key and this gave him additional facility and showed new possibilities for use when playing in the more usual jazz keys of F, B♭ and C (in the same way as control on extremely fast tempos gives one additional possibilities when playing slow).

He was heavily influenced by Lester Young, saxophonist with the

Count Basie Band. Young, in contrast to the hard, brash sound of tenor saxophonists like Coleman Hawkins, the generally accepted style of the time, tried to get a softer sound, more indeed like an alto saxophone. In his solos Young was more adventurous than many of his contemporaries, playing across the beat and normal phrase lines and using upper extensions of chords. He also played on ballads beautifully, believing that one must know the lyrics of a song before one can improvise on it effectively. It was these extensions to the jazz language, linked with those shown by Charlie Christian, a young guitarist with Benny Goodman, that developed into the music we know as bop – a music in which Parker's voice predominated.

Bop, from rebop or bebop, onomatopoeic expressions of the sounds used in the new music, changed the language of jazz radically. The period leading up to this change (the 1930s) was known as the swing era and was the time jazz reached its peak of popularity. The accent on a soloist with supporting rhythm structure – pioneered by Louis Armstrong – as distinct from the collective improvisation of earlier groups, had become commonplace. The essential difference though, was that the supporting structure as well as coming from the rhythm section came from groups of instruments (saxophone, trumpets or trombones) playing repetitive patterns known as riffs. Many of the big bands employed the call and response patterns of the Negro preachers with the soloist answering the band's phrases or vice versa. The harmonies were very basic, often the 12-bar blues, the rhythmic pulse was a very heavy 4 in a bar and the main desire of the band was to swing and generate excitement in the audience. The coming of bop changed all this: melodic lines became more complex, often sounding like written down improvisations instead of essentially rhythmically based melodic motifs; harmonies were altered vertically, by adding extensions and altering basic chord notes, and horizontally, by the use of passing chords and substitute chords. The basic pulse became lighter, being based on a cymbal statement of the time ♩ ♫ ♩ ♫ instead of a pounding bass drum beat ♩ ♩ ♩ ♩ This latter change had the effect of freeing the string bass from its purely supporting role to a more flowing harmonically based line. (The only area of jazz left unaltered by the changes of bop was the overall form, still largely a matter of theme – solos – theme.)

Solo styles also altered following the seeds shown in the work of Young and Christian and the pioneering of Parker who tells how, when playing 'Cherokee', he suddenly hit on the idea of playing the upper extensions of the chords as a melody line. This follows on the more basic chord-orientated improvising of the swing era musicians. Another change was the shift from a crotchet (quarter note) based improvising – where the main note values used were ♪ ♩ ♩ – to a quaver (8th note) based music with ♪♪ ♩ being the main values used.

As with swing era improvising though, bop improvisers like Parker tended to ignore the given melody when constructing their improvisations. This is not to say that the solos are unmelodic. Parker can often be heard constructing a solo from one simple melodic motif (as for example in 'Embraceable You') altering it rhythmically and melodically to fit the changing harmonies underneath. Parker's solos were good compositions – but composed instantly.

His tone on the alto was more intense than had been heard in jazz, where the more lyrical sound of Johnny Hodges was the norm. Like Hodges though, Parker was a passionate player and his solos have a searing intensity that makes you believe in every note he plays. Marshall Stearns described them as possessing a 'tortured, searing, blasting beauty'. Many of his solos almost burst at the seams in his effort to cram all his experience into that one solo and often his solo entries seem uncontrollable as he comes exploding in. His solos were also heavily blues influenced, even his versions of standard songs are, as Francis Newton says, 'the unadulterated lowest of lowdown blues'.

Parker and other composers in the bop period often took the chord progressions of standard songs and wrote new melodies over them. Such melodies often look like written out improvisations and are quite tricky to play, 'Donna Lee' for example. Such famous jazz tunes as 'Anthropology', 'Oleo' and 'Salt Peanuts' are all based on the chords of 'I Got Rhythm'; 'Ornithology' on 'How High The Moon'; and 'Donna Lee' on 'Indiana'. But, as has been mentioned, such melodies had little effect on the actual solo. They were used simply as 'launching pads' to set up a chord progression, a tempo and a mood. In many of Parker's theme statements he paraphrases the melody and improvises quite extensively around that melody as though he can't wait to get into the improvising proper. This also explains why the bop composers wrote new tunes on standard chord sequences. If they were going to interpret the melody so freely and only really use the chord progression, then why not think up a fresh version of the tune and thereby collect the composer royalties themselves?

Parker played and recorded extensively in the forties, most often with Dizzy Gillespie (a trumpet player of phenomenal technique who was also highly influential in the development of bop) but sometimes with the very young, still developing trumpeter Miles Davis who rarely sounded happy in the bop situation. Most of the recordings were with the classic bop instrumentation of alto, trumpet, piano, bass and drums, and using the accepted jazz form of theme–solos– theme on a 12-bar blues or 32-bar standard. Parker, who had developed an interest in straight music, grew increasingly dissatisfied with these limitations and made arrangements to study with Edgar Varèse. He also admired the German composer Paul Hindemith greatly and said that he 'would like to emulate the precise, complex harmonic structures of Hindemith but with an emotional colouring and dynamic shading that modern classical music lacks'.

The plans to study with Varèse were never followed through because of Parker's death and the only time he recorded outside the normal jazz situation was a rather syrupy string album made largely for commercial reasons by promoter Norman Granz. Parker played jazz in spite of the unsympathetic background but he sounds quite inhibited and never really gets as passionately involved as he normally did. It is ironic that this was one of the sessions most liked by Parker, a normally extremely self-critical musician who, one suspects, was overawed by the new-found 'respectability' of his surroundings.

Parker's death was attributed to lobar pneumonia but there is no doubt that his addiction to heroin and his large consumption of alcohol played its part. This combination of the two is rare, in that an addiction to heroin usually creates an aversion to alcohol. (Heroin came into use during the Second World War. Before that jazz musicians, in common with all other people searching for stimulants, used softer drugs like marijuana or drank heavily. Many bop musicians, though, believed that alcohol made a musician sloppy and preferred the 'cleaner' heroin. They forgot – or didn't care to remember – that though alcohol *may* lead to addiction in the form of alcoholism, heroin *almost inevitably* leads to addiction and death.)

Parker, unlike most addicts, functioned comparatively normally for a large proportion of the time. His appetites for food, sex and alcohol, normally affected heavily by heroin addiction, were unimpaired. Surprisingly also, he often played well while under the influence but often the craving took over and the necessity to 'score' (find his drugs) became the most urgent task of the day. Like all addicts he believed that he could kick it at will, but inevitably it became his master, and ultimately his art suffered. Possibly though,

Parker without drugs would have been unable to face the creative pressures he was under . . . The question is unanswerable, though certainly none who tried to emulate him *through* drugs attained the same level of achievement. One must simply accept that Parker was unique – a man like Armstrong who altered the complete direction of jazz; but, unlike Armstrong, he killed himself doing so.

REFERENCES

LISTENING : BOP RECORDS

Parker recorded with most of the famous bop musicians such as Dizzy Gillespie, Thelonius Monk, Bud Powell, Max Roach, etc., and these are listed in the General section following.
Charlie Christian – 'Solo Flight', *Anthology*.
Lester Young – 'Oh, Lady Be Good' and 'Tickletoe', *Anthology*.
Coleman Hawkins – 'Jamaica Shout', *Anthology*.
Parker with strings – *The Definitive Charlie Parker* (Metro), Volumes 1 and 5.

FURTHER READING

Swing era – Chapter 13, 'The big band'.
The blues feel – Chapter 10, 'The blues'.
Chord progressions – Chapter 11, 'The popular song form'.
Kansas City – *Jazz Style in Kansas City and the South West* by Ross Russell (California U.P., 1971).

PROJECTS

Kansas City
Comparison of sax sounds – Lester Young and Coleman Hawkins; Johnny Hodges, Charlie Parker and Ornette Coleman; John Surman and Harry Carney.
Does it *matter* what sort of man Parker was? Was his art better or worse because of his addiction? Does it show in his music – for better or worse? (There might be a useful comparison here with Rimbaud and others.)

GENERAL

POINTS TO LISTEN FOR

1. the emotion and intensity of his playing
2. the flow of notes – floats across the beat; across the bar line and 'phrase line', and across chorus breaks

3. the complexity of rhythmic superimpositions

4. the dense harmonic structures

5. the often complex initial theme statements.

(Note that Charlie Parker's style is relatively harder to listen to than, say, Miles Davis or Louis Armstrong. A possible easy way in would be via the string tracks where he is fairly inhibited and is playing on standard songs where other versions could be compared.)

SUGGESTED RECORDS (best period 1945–54)

Quintet of the Year (Saga-Pan). Recorded live in Toronto, 1953, with five of the finest bop musicians – Parker, Gillespie, Mingus, Bud Powell and Max Roach. Brilliant playing.

Loverman (Realm). Recorded 1946 when he was very ill, but the raw intensity of the man comes through in a disturbing way.

The Pick of Parker and *The Essential C.P.* (Verve). Selective tracks living up to their titles as 'essential'.

(Many Parker recordings have alternative takes, of interest when studying solos in depth but of little overall interest. The ones mentioned above are all best takes.)

FURTHER READING

Bird Lives by Ross Russell (Quartet Books, 1972). Biography of Parker by his one time recording manager. Brilliant and one of the best musical biographies written.

Bird by Robert Reisner (Quartet, 1974). Recollections by family and friends.

Jazz, its Evolution and Essence, chapter 7.

5 Miles Davis

His position as a catalyst

Though jazz fans and critics are renowned for elevating merely good musicians to 'genius' standard it would seem that there are three uncontestable geniuses in jazz; Louis Armstrong, who moved jazz from the collective improvisation of the New Orleans style to its status as a soloist's art – an art capable of expressing personal emotion; Charlie Parker, who revitalised the language of jazz in the mid-forties, and Duke Ellington, who found a way of incorporating the improvisatory qualities of jazz into composition. The trumpeter Miles Davis is a strong contender for inclusion with this select group. He is one of the few musicians to be a commercial success without compromising his remarkable talent and he has been tremendously important to jazz as a catalyst, first for the west coast developments of the late 1940s, then for the utilisation of modes in the late 1950s. He was also the focal point for what André Hodier described as 'the rebirth of the Ellington spirit' in his work with Gil Evans, and he has been largely responsible for the jazz–rock movement which started in the middle 1960s. His influence is apparent on almost all contemporary trumpet players as well as many other instrumentalists, and many of the important figures in contemporary jazz have passed through his various bands. He is perhaps the only musician in jazz who has been creative in so many different environments and who continues to surprise us with his further explorations.

Miles Davis was born in 1926 in Alton, Illinois. He went to New York to study at the Juilliard School of Music but left after deciding he could learn more by listening to and playing with Charlie Parker. He recorded with Parker before he was twenty-one but never sounded completely happy in the complexities of bop. He lacked range and instrumental technique – particularly when compared with Parker or Dizzy Gillespie, whose technical expertise were at that time affecting all instrumentalists. What he did possess though was a sense of structure in his solos and the beginnings of a passionate lyricism which was soon to develop further, although like many young soloists he had to learn the value of space and his technical problems were not fully mastered until the early 1960s. His tone was nearly vibrato-less; he had been told by an early teacher that 'You're going to get old anyway and start shaking, so don't cultivate a vibrato now.'

In 1948 Davis organised a nine-piece band and although the group only played two weeks in public its influence, through the recordings it made, has been enormous. It was the first time that the musical advances of bop, the more interesting harmonies and more complex melodic lines, had been applied to a larger group of instruments than the conventional bop quintet, and the Davis band and the arrangers concerned took full advantage of the possibilities offered by the unusual instrumentation – trumpet and trombone, alto and baritone saxes, french horn and tuba, and the conventional rhythm section of piano, bass and drums. This line-up was chosen to give the writers maximum possibilities with the smallest possible group of musicians and was heavily influenced by the band of Claud Thornhill, a well-known dance band of the time with which many of the personnel had worked. They utilised the Ellingtonian concept of treating instruments individually, of blending sounds and using instruments in fresh situations. The french horn was usually given the dissonance of the chord because of its ability to blend with other instruments, and the tuba was used as a melodic instrument rather than in its old-fashioned role of bass. Instruments were also used in the extremes of their ranges, thus providing chords with a slight edge. A trombone on his high B♭ will give a different effect in a chord than an alto sax on the same note.

It is appropriate that the album made by the band should have become known as *The Birth of The Cool* because connected with the band – and influenced by it – were many of the people later to be associated with the so-called cool school of jazz on the west coast of America. These included Gerry Mulligan, who later expanded on these concepts in his own groups – first his pianoless quartet with trumpeter Chet Baker and later in his big bands; John Lewis, now musical director of the Modern Jazz Quartet, a group which again stems from the same ideas; Lee Konitz, a very thin-toned alto player who refined the 'cool' concepts to an almost arid style, and Gunther Schuller, composer and author of *Early Jazz* and responsible for many of the third stream developments which attempted to merge jazz with straight music.

Miles Davis

Perhaps the most important member of the band though was Gil Evans, a Canadian arranger who had worked with Claud Thornhill for eight years where he had arranged many of Charlie Parker's tunes for the band. Such performances nearly always contained a remarkable final chorus – a kind of arranger's improvisation – which has seldom been equalled. Ten years after *Birth of the Cool* he again recorded with Davis and the three albums they made together, *Miles Ahead*, *Porgy and Bess* and *Sketches of Spain* are justifiably rated as among the best records in the whole of jazz. There is a strong Ellington influence throughout these albums both in the orchestration, though a larger group of instruments was used than Ellington normally had and instruments such as french horn, oboe, harp and bassoon were used, and in the concerto-like placing of the soloist against the orchestra. It seems though that there is something lacking: there is a surface glibness; a concentration on *clothing* Davis's contribution rather than adding to it. Ideally the jazz composer should make the player play beyond himself, be inspired to express an emotion of which he is perhaps unaware at the time. In the main, beautiful as they are, these three albums fail to do that, though there are hints of what could have been in 'Saeta' (*Sketches of Spain*) and 'Prayer' (*Porgy and Bess*), but it took Evans several years from being 'simply' a good orchestrator to become a good *composer* also.

REFERENCES

LISTENING

With Parker – *Charlie Parker On Dial* (Spotlite), Volumes 4, 5, 6.
Claude Thornhill Band – 'Yardbird Suite', *Anthology*.
    Birth of the Cool (Capitol).
Gerry Mulligan Quartet – 'As Catch Can', *Anthology*.
Gerry Mulligan Big Band – *Concert in Jazz* (Verve).
John Lewis and the MJQ – *The Art of the MJQ* (Atlantic).
Lee Konitz – 'Yardbird Suite', *Anthology*.
Gunther Schuller – *Jazz Abstractions* (Atlantic). Contains variations of 'Django' and 'Criss Cross'.
With Gil Evans – *Miles Ahead* (CBS). Suite, mostly of others' tunes, but recomposed and orchestrated by Evans into continuous piece. Features Davis on flugelhorn. Includes a version of Delibes' 'Maids of Cadiz'.
    Porgy and Bess (CBS). Evans' version of Gershwin score which he studied thoroughly. 'Summertime' is interesting in its variations in texture on the one accompanying riff and 'Prayer' for the 'preaching' role of Davis.

Sketches of Spain (CBS). Includes 'Saeta' (a representation of a Spanish religious procession where Davis takes the part of a hondo singer). Also includes the adagio from 'Concierto de Aranjuez' for guitar and orchestra by Joaquin Rodrigo. Davis plays around the original guitar part.
Later Gil Evans – 'El Toreador' on *The Individualism of Gil Evans*.
'Lotus Land' on *Guitar Forms*, Kenny Burrell. (Both Verve.)
Svengali (Atlantic).

FURTHER READING

Birth of the Cool – Jazz, its Evolution and Essence, chapter 8.

PROJECTS

Study of the concerto – In straight music and in jazz (mainly Ellington, 'Concerto for Cootie' and 'Clarinet Lament' for example, and Evans); compare the Evans version of 'Concierto de Aranjuez' with the original.
Re-composition – Evans' versions of 'Concierto de Aranjuez' and standard tunes are really re-compositions, *new* versions rather than just arrangements. Compare variations in straight music.
Comparison of versions – Of the *Porgy and Bess* original; of Delibes' 'Maids of Cadiz' (on *Miles Ahead*).

New possibilities in improvising

Davis's own playing on the albums with Evans was brilliant but in the early fifties it had been erratic mainly because of his addiction to heroin. But he cured it and from that time on his playing was revitalised. His tone became fuller – more intense and passionate; he learnt to use space, to know where to rest, where to leave gaps. His recordings of that period showed a much more mature solo style – he was supremely confident and even the fluffs which he still made, seemed unimportant. He returned to public notice with a wildly acclaimed performance at the 1955 Newport Jazz Festival, and during the middle and late fifties made a series of brilliant recordings with a quintet which included the tenor saxophonist John Coltrane – whose later work was of great importance to jazz. It was this group, with the addition of Cannonball Adderly on alto sax, that made the *Kind of Blue* album in 1958. This record was prompted by Davis's work with Gil Evans and had a revolutionary impact on jazz.

By the mid-fifties many jazz musicians were tiring of the melodic and harmonic complexities of bop, and of the phony pseudo-gospel sounds of the 'funky' hard-bop groups that had followed. Parker himself had expressed dissatisfaction with the forms used in jazz (12-bar blues or 32-bar standard songs with theme–solos–theme development) but little attempt was made to get away from them until, working completely independently, Miles Davis and Ornette Coleman discovered new methods.

Davis felt that the 32-bar chord progression was restricting, particularly when the movements between the chords and the chords themselves were as complex as they had become in bop. He simplified matters by using scales for improvisation, reasoning that the simplicity of the scale would force soloists to work melodically rather than harmonically. He had prophesied earlier that 'there will be fewer chords but infinite possibilities as to what to do with them'. For the *Kind of Blue* recording sessions Davis brought along various extensions of this idea. In 'Flamenco Sketches' each soloist is given five scales and plays on each scale until he wants to move. In 'So What' Davis uses a standard AABA 32-bar song form but his melodic material and improvising is based on the Dorian mode (the C scale starting on D) which is transposed a semitone for the B part of the form.

Two of Davis's 'infinite possibilities' can be seen by comparing the improvisations on *Kind of Blue* – particularly 'So What' – of Davis and John Coltrane. Davis is very lyrical, playing basically around the available notes – working *within* the scale. Coltrane is much more complex rhythmically and melodically – working *from* the scale – and he is seemingly feeling his way to the aptly titled 'sheets of sound' approach he used in later years, where he seems to want to get all the notes into every chord.

Kind of Blue appears to be in isolation as Davis returned after that to playing standard song material. His approach, though, had altered and he was much freer with his given material. If one compares versions of standard songs ('My Funny Valentine' and 'Stella by Starlight' are good examples) before and after *Kind of Blue* there is a vast difference. Before, the tunes are played fairly straight and the solos follow a strict chorus shape. Afterwards, taking advantage of the freedoms shown by his modal experiments, Davis seems to *re-compose* the material, taking it apart chord by chord and phrase by phrase. There is no dividing line between theme statement and solo, they blur into each other and the whole becomes much more than a jazz musician playing a known melody. They point the way to a possible new language in jazz – intensely personal reshapings of standard compositions which seem, by their perfection, to have been meticulously composed rather than improvised on the spot.

Having shown new possibilities in dealing with the standard song, Miles Davis turned his attention to original compositions – not necessarily his own but often those of other members of his band. This trend has been common to most jazz groups since the early 1960s. Many of these compositions incorporated the modal develop-ments of *Kind of Blue*, others utilised various aspects of the other main stream of jazz experimentation which developed into what is known as the avant garde. Chief among these developments was a much freer use of the rhythm section. The pulse was often implied rather than actually stated, and if it was stated it was by the bass player rather than the drummer, who was left much freer to concentrate on *colour* and the creation of tension. The drums moved up with the front line soloing instruments and there was no longer the division between soloist and rhythm section instruments. Melodies were much more angular and sketchier and again things were implied rather than stated. Harmonies were often modal, or used chords in a freer and usually simpler way than those of the bop period. Most important jazz became a *group* adventure again, with all members being equal. There was a change from the soloist and support idea which had ruled in jazz since Armstrong.

REFERENCES

LISTENING

Rebirth of Miles Davis – *Walkin'* (Prestige). Includes J. J. Johnson, Lucky Thompson, Horace Silver.
With John Coltrane – *Milestones* (CBS).
   'Sweet Sue' and 'Two Bass Hit', *Anthology*.
Kind of Blue (CBS). Note, there is a mislabelling on some records. 'Flamenco Sketches' is track 2.
Free rhythm section – *Nefertiti* (CBS). Title track has repeating melody throughout while rhythm section improvise around it. The melody itself is played very freely with one player often echoing the other.

FURTHER READING

On contemporary developments – Chapter 16, 'Contemporary trends', Chapter 14, 'Modes and scales'.

Comparative versions of well-known tunes (either by the same or different players). Miles Davis recorded several different versions of many standards, such as 'My Funny Valentine', 'Stella by Starlight', 'Bye Bye Blackbird'.

Electric instruments in jazz

In the mid-sixties Miles Davis started experimenting with electric instruments and rock sounds. Historically this links up with the emergence of rock – from rhythm and blues – as a strong part of the contemporary music scene. It had an increasing influence on jazz and many groups adopted rock rhythms and rock instruments into their music. At times this was done for commercial ends – cashing in on rock music – but it rarely worked and usually ended up as a hybrid music between the two. Davis though started to use the instruments and sounds as colour to add to his usual sounds and tunes. Instead of a regular jazz pulse around the 4 beats in a bar ♩ ♩ ♩ ♩ | ♩ ♩ ♩ ♩ he had an 8 in the bar feel in the drums ♫♫♫♫ ♫♫♫♫ | ♫♫♫♫ ♫♫♫♫. In place of the regular string bass and piano on some numbers he used the electric bass and an electric piano.

Electric sounds were not of course new in jazz but had been generally limited to the occasional use of organ and the use of the amplified or electric guitar. This came into jazz in the mid 1930s when Eddie Durham (after first using a tin resonator) used an electrically amplified instrument with the Jimmie Lunceford band. At that time the role of the guitar was as part of the rhythm section providing a steady unobtrusive 4 beats to a bar, and it was amplified in order that it would cut through the sound of the big band. Amplification led to the emergence of the guitar as a solo instrument in the swing era, particularly with the work of Charlie Christian who, although he died at the age of twenty-two of TB, was a very great influence on guitar styles, concentrating on single note playing as opposed to chords, and on the development of bop.

The bass guitar came into jazz directly from and because of rock. It differs from the regular string bass in that it is fretted and the space between the notes is much closer, making intonation easier and fast passages easier to finger. Its sound can be varied by use of the amplifier controls but the instrument is more often used for volume than good sound quality.

The electric piano seems to have come into contemporary music, rock and jazz, almost simultaneously in an attempt to make the organ more like a regular piano. Such efforts were prompted by the dissatisfaction musicians expressed about the state of repair of many ordinary pianos, now referred to as 'acoustic' or 'steam' pianos, and the fact that it was often very difficult to hear them against drummers, who became increasingly loud as the rock influence took hold. The instrument at its best is like a cross between a well amplified guitar and a good acoustic piano.

At first Miles Davis and other bands in jazz were using these sounds purely as colour, rather as in earlier days jazz groups had added Latin American rhythms and instruments to their music. A new direction was shown on Miles Davis's record *In A Silent Way* where the rock instruments, *three* electric pianos and guitar plus string bass and drums, all working within clearly defined limits, were used to provide a carpet of sound for the soloists. *In A Silent Way* was important as well in that it was one of the first jazz records to be heavily edited after recording. Such practices are usually confined to joining between alternate takes to include a better solo or to take out a mistake. In this record and the subsequent *Bitches Brew* the editing takes over. Theme statements and solos are repeated by editing them in and the music becomes manipulated by the engineers rather than created by the musicians.

On *Bitches Brew* Davis used an echo device to provide new effects and subsequently has used electronic gadgetry more associated with rock guitarists than jazz horn players. He used direct amplification by contact mike plus a 'wah wah pedal' and a 'fuzz box'. Both increase the tonal possibilities but are often over-used.

The use of such gadgetry in his records and public appearances has alienated many of Davis's staunch fans – although it gained him an increased audience of new, younger fans mostly from rock. Musicians have gradually come to accept *Bitches Brew* but have, in the main, drawn the line at the later performances where themes and arrangements are dispensed with. The carpet of sound approach has been augmented, usually with extra percussion such as conga players, and Davis's own solos have often seemed cursory with little trace of his previous magic. He has, according to many observers, lost his identity in a morass of percussion and gadgetry, but there are signs that he knows *exactly* what he is doing and is once again exploring new frontiers in jazz. Certainly on the strength of his past record it is difficult to ignore whatever he chooses to do.

Miles Davis now has the status of a super-star. He appears regularly at venues and festivals more associated with pop and rock than jazz, and has a life-style – Lamborghini car, private boxing instructor, property investments – more in keeping with a rich young lawyer than a jazz musician. He generally ignores his audience almost completely and never announces the personnel of his band, nor the names of the pieces he is playing. He has always surrounded himself with brilliant young musicians and expects the public to buy his records and therefore know who is in the band and what he is playing without the formality of announcements. Like a true super-star he displays a cool arrogance to his audience and his critics and his comment on a woman who 'didn't understand' a performance of his is typical (and carries a great deal of truth): 'It took me twenty years' study and practice to work up to what I wanted to play in this performance. How can she expect to listen five minutes and understand it?'

REFERENCES

LISTENING

Use of electric instruments – *In a Silent Way* (CBS).
　Bitches Brew (CBS).
Later records – *On the Corner* (CBS).
　In Concert (CBS).
Contemporary rock groups using jazz and vice versa – Cream, Soft Machine,
　John McLaughlin's Mahavishnu Orchestra, Blood, Sweat and Tears,
　and Nucleus.

FURTHER READING

On recording – *Inside Jazz*, pp. 133–40, gives an account of the various
　recording processes (recording, mixing and editing).

PROJECTS

On the morality of editing – Is it right to edit between different performances?
　To use the devices possible in a studio to change the musical sound,
　especially if it can't be re-created in concert? (This last point applies to
　rock and pop also.)
On continuing faith in an artist – Should one continue to believe in an
　artist's integrity after he has produced several bad records, particularly
　if, like Miles Davis, he has had so much previous success and influence?

On understanding art – Is it necessary to understand a piece of art to enjoy it?
Do you increase your enjoyment the more you know about it?

GENERAL

POINTS TO LISTEN FOR

1. his lyricism
2. his use of space in his solos – and their architecture
3. (in later recordings) use of entire range of the trumpet
4. the quality of the other musicians in his bands
5. the variety of sounds and range of dynamics used.

SUGGESTED RECORDS (no particular best period)

Birth of the Cool (CBS)
Kind of Blue (CBS)
Sketches of Spain (CBS)
The Essential Miles Davis (3 records, CBS). Includes 'All Blues' (from *Kind of Blue*), 'Springsville' and 'Maids of Cadiz' (from *Miles Ahead*), 'Concierto de Aranjuez' (from *Sketches of Spain*), 'Summertime' (from *Porgy and Bess*), 'My Funny Valentine' (from *Lincoln Centre*) and a track from *Bitches Brew*.

FURTHER READING

No biographies available.

Dave Brubeck

6 Dave Brubeck

The problem of status

Jazz has always had an ambivalent position in society. At first it was predominantly a negro music, a strong part of the fabric of life in New Orleans but considered a novelty by the rest of the world. As it spread it became an entertainment music, with the swing era big bands providing the popular music of the day, but there was always an air of 'sin' and 'danger' attached to it. With the emergence of bop the music altered and changed from being art as entertainment to art as art – but an art that was forced to take place mainly in bars and night clubs. Since that time jazz has become more accepted. It is often played in concert halls and receives a small body of subsidy, but it has rarely achieved respectability and there is often still a feeling of condescension in public attitudes towards jazz. Jazz musicians are just not considered to be the same status as straight musicians. They are rarely considered for cultural exchanges, and jazz is not always treated as an art form by the media. While many straight avant garde musicians can attract large fees for their world-wide concert appearances, avant garde jazz musicians like Cecil Taylor have difficulty in finding engagements.

It is not surprising then that many jazz musicians consciously or subconsciously strive for such stature, seeking the position in society that their straight music equivalents have. This may simply be a matter of presentation – of dressing up in morning suits and conforming to concert hall stage manners as the Modern Jazz Quartet used to. It may lead to the addition of straight music devices such as fugue and canon, or it may lead to the desire to play with a vast string section as did Charlie Parker when he recorded for promoter Norman Granz in 1949. Granz stated that 'Parker for the first time plays with truly great musicians'! This comment, after Parker had played for years with such bop stars as Dizzy Gillespie and Bud Powell, shows that the quest for status – and its attendant snobbery – did not only come from musicians. It may be the wish to re-arrange a straight composition with

61

jazz colourings or use 'orchestral' instruments such as harp or cello. All these devices are often used in the hope that they will make their music – and themselves – more respectable while still jazz.

The Modern Jazz Quartet are one of the few groups in jazz who have achieved such respectability and stature without, in the main, lessening the quality of their work. Most of the other musicians and groups who have sought such status have achieved it at the expense of their jazz talent or have been given the respectability because of the easy appeal of the well packaged but mainly superficial music they play. Such a group is that of pianist Dave Brubeck.

Brubeck was born in 1920 (the same year as Charlie Parker) in Concord, California. He is, after Louis Armstrong and Duke Ellington, perhaps the best known jazz musician in the world but is regrettably far below them in musical stature. He studied under Darius Milhaud and, briefly, with Arnold Schoenberg. His first band was an octet, formed around the time of Miles Davis's *Birth of the Cool* sessions, but lacking their orchestral textures. Its aim was said to be 'to contain, at its best, the vigour and force of simple jazz, the harmonic complexities of Bartok and Milhaud, the form (and much of the dignity) of Bach, and at times the lyrical romanticism of Rachmaninov'. Not unexpectedly it failed.

His quartet was formed in 1951 and his popularity was established with his concert appearances, particularly those in colleges; he was the first jazz musician to break into this market. His recordings in the fifties (often of such college concerts) contained many standard songs such as 'I Want to Be Happy' and 'The Song is You' but his big breakthrough was his recording of 'Take Five' – a composition in 5/4 and one of the first pieces in jazz outside the regular 4/4, or much less common 3/4, pulse. Strange as it seems now perhaps, this record did get into the Top Twenty and many people were heard whistling the theme. The rhythm of 'Take Five' ♪♩ ♪♩ ♩ ♩ was insistently played throughout. It was the anchoring point for the players and very necessary at the time, but nowadays these new times are much more common and such 'hypnotic' rhythms can be played more subtly, if not dispensed with altogether.

The composer of 'Take Five' was Paul Desmond, the alto saxophone player with Brubeck's group, and one of the few post-Parker saxophonists who did not sound like Parker. His sound was much thinner and cooler and was often criticised (Eddie Condon, an outspoken guitarist of the Chicago era, said he sounded 'like a female alcoholic'), but his style was very fluid and he seems to create an effortless flow of good improvised melodies. He can often be heard playing duets with himself by alternating phrases in his upper and lower registers. There is no doubt that he made an enormous contribution to the success of the Brubeck Quartet, both for his own solos and for the improvised duets he went into with Dave Brubeck.

Brubeck's own solos though are rarely fluid. They fail to swing and often conclude with a great series of crashing chords, like high-note trumpet solos and drum solos, great crowd pleasers but of little jazz value. He is essentially a harmonic and rhythmic player rather than a melodist like Desmond and he will often be self-consciously clever, injecting into his playing such devices as improvised quasi-fugues or canons, or playing superimpositions of different rhythms in each hand.

A comparison between Brubeck and Desmond will, on most tunes, serve to demonstrate the meaning of swing and the difference between very good and merely adequate improvising. Desmond, a wry-humoured man who once expressed surprise at the constant stage smiles of the other members of the group saying 'no one can be *that* happy', has expressed satisfaction with Brubeck's 'comping' (from 'complementing' – meaning the way a pianist accompanies a soloist). He says that Brubeck does not simply play for himself as many pianists do but tries to complement: to assist the soloist.

A rather unexpected champion of Brubeck as pianist is Cecil Taylor, an extremely gifted and technically brilliant avant garde pianist. He says – and he is one of the very few to admit it – that he has been influenced by Brubeck, being impressed by 'the depth and texture of his harmony'.

The rhythm section of most of Dave Brubeck's various groups, excepting the one with Alan Dawson on drums, often seem to be too polite – there is no guts or drive; superficially because the drummer uses brushes often and the bass revolves around 2 beats in a bar, but the overall impression of the Brubeck Quartet (apart from some of Paul Desmond's solo work) is lack of involvement. Although one must assume everyone is trying the feeling remains that it is all superficial. One misses the intensity, the passion, the sheer *involvement* in every note they play, of an Armstrong, a Parker or a Davis.

REFERENCES

LISTENING

Modern Jazz Quartet – *The Art of the MJQ* (Atlantic).
'Take Five' on *Dave Brubeck's Greatest Hits* (CBS).
Cecil Taylor – *Nuits de la Foundation Maeght*, Volumes 1 and 2 (Shandar, France).
'Waltz Limps' on the *Anthology* contains some awkward sounding super-impositions of time.

FURTHER READING

The 'status' situation in Britain – *Inside Jazz*.
  Music Outside by Ian Carr (Latimer Press, 1973).
On new times – Chapter 16, 'Contemporary trends'.

PROJECTS

Intensity, involvement and indifference. Richard Burton said once that the worst crime of all was indifference. That it was better to be bad and mean it than just indifferent. Discuss.

Jazzing the classics

Like many jazz musicians Dave Brubeck has become involved from time to time in what has become known as 'jazzing the classics' – presenting jazz versions of classical themes. In his case he chose not Bach, who has long been pilloried in this way, most notably by Jacques Loussier whose Play Bach concerts and records are wildly popular and highly boring, but Mozart. He re-arranged Mozart's 'Turkish Rondo' in 9/8 (2 2 2 3 instead of the usual 3 3 3) and re-christened it 'Blue Rondo à la Turk'. Like 'Take Five' it was very successful but unlike 'Take Five' it sounds forced – the rhythms seem self-conscious, rather like his use of clever devices in solos. The whole piece has an air of 'look how clever we are, we can play Mozart but *we* do it in 9/8'. The fact that the jazz solos are played, not in Mozart's chord structure, but on the old standby of the blues, and not in 9/8 but in 4/4, is, I feel, not insignificant. It is rather as though, having satisfied respectability by using Mozart, and cleverness by putting it in 9/8, he felt he could then relax into ordinary jazz. The result is an unsatisfactory hybrid.

Much more satisfactory have been Brubeck's own compositions, at least his small form pieces. Many of his melodies have been played and recorded by other jazz musicians ('The Duke' for example is on the Gil Evans/Miles Davis *Miles Ahead* album, and Bill Evans has recorded 'In Your Own Sweet Way') and such tunes are now recognised jazz standards. Some of these good tunes crop up in his series of 'Jazz Impressions of . . .' suites but many of the tunes suffer from too much surface colour from whatever area he is meant to be depicting. Even the most successful pieces though serve to emphasise the problems of programme music in jazz. 'Plain Song' for example, from Brubeck's *Jazz Impressions of the USA*, has a lost, desolate feel to the melody and the accompanying simple bass figure. Desmond, because of his tone quality (and talent as an improviser) seems able to retain and indeed develop the mood while Brubeck himself is less convincing, often slipping into his own mannerisms and seeming far too self-conscious about the ideas he is using to capture the mood. It would seem essential that if such programme music is to work effectively in jazz that the soloist is carefully chosen for his ability to express and, ideally, build on the particular mood chosen by the composer, and that the accompanying rhythm pattern and counterlines if used should continue that mood. Too often a theme will portray a place or an idea but the solos which follow, though they may be good in isolation, do nothing to continue or develop the mood and content of the original idea.

Brubeck's longer compositions have generally suffered from the pretentiousness that he exhibits in his own playing. They can be categorised as belonging in the so-called third stream (a term coined by Gunther Schuller to describe 'a music that attempts to fuse the essential characteristics of jazz and so-called classical music') and like most such pieces they *lose* the essential character of jazz while failing to put anything in its place. The jazz content is confined to a steady pulse and some syncopations in the writing and the improvised solos are seemingly added as an afterthought. At its best there would seem to be an uneasy blend between the two elements, at its worst it sounds, as someone once said, like two nearby radio stations merging together. Brubeck's 'Light in the Wilderness, an Oratorio for Today' exhibits the worst excesses of such writing. The parts for full orchestra are often naïve and the jazz improvising, seemingly an afterthought, is poor. This piece though – and many similar pieces – have been popular and widened the audience for Brubeck's music. They have also made him more accepted as a 'respectable' jazz musician but provide further examples of status being achieved at the expense of musical content.

The musical reason for such failures is often, sadly, a lack of compositional talent in the composers. Linked with this however – and perhaps an explanation why many good composers fail – are three points.

First, the insistence of many such writers that the jazz feel is primarily one of pulse: that whatever notes and rhythms are written they will automatically become jazz if they are put over a ♩ ♩ ♩ ♩ ♩ ♩ | ♩ cymbal beat.

Second, the failure to make improvisation an integral part of the piece: it is usually grafted on later with the soloist almost chosen at random, rather than carefully selected for what he can add.

Third, the necessity for jazz composers to think of their musicians as individuals, and the equal necessity for the players to know each other, both near impossibilities with large groups of players.

These would also seem to be the reasons why large string sections have rarely worked in jazz. Some of the more commercial efforts are pleasant, but here the very nature of the writing is for an anonymous mass rather than individuals and works better when the soloist is soft and melodic like Paul Desmond, rather than angular and abrasive like Charlie Parker. As well as the matter of the individuality of the musicians there is the question of phrasing. Strings do not, particularly when in a mass, 'swing' in the same way as a jazz rhythm section does. They tend to lag fractionally behind the beat whereas the jazz players always push ahead, and for this reason the placing of a string section over a 4 beats to a bar rhythm section rarely works effectively. Also the actual writing for the strings is often heavy and graceless, relying on sustained harmonies for its effect. The result is that the strings seem to act like syrup – slowly clogging up the works. This peculiarity of strings in jazz was utilised brilliantly in Danish composer Palle Mikkelborg's suite 'The Mysterious Corona' where he seemed to seek this effect *deliberately* and had the rhythm section disintegrate into confusion, apparently overwhelmed by the weight of the strings.

At the time of writing the only completely successful jazz album with strings has been Eddie Sauter's *Focus*, featuring Stan Getz. Sauter, who had previously worked for Benny Goodman, realised that contemporary composers such as Bartok and Stravinsky had made their music swing by the *attack* of the strings and the rhythms they used. He therefore dispensed with the conventional rhythm section, only using a drummer on one track – and then in a free improvisatory way rather than simply as a time-keeper. He also used as cornerstones of his small string section the members of the Beaux Arts Quartet who of course had the affinity, the ease of working together, of a good small jazz group. Stan Getz's role as soloist is interesting in that he was asked to improvise around the strings, to listen to what they were doing and to create a new layer of sound which complemented theirs. And this without being told in which specific areas to play or rest. He plays magnificently.

The question of subsidy

Unfortunately neither of these unique concepts – the effective use of strings without a conventional rhythm section and the freely roaming improviser over a composed backing – has been explored further. One reason is economics. To set up a large orchestra for a concert or a recording is expensive and although a Brubeck or a Getz may persuade a record company or a concert promoter to put on such a venture, most other musicians have to rely on subsidy. This form of support is becoming increasingly common in jazz but is still insufficient for the current state of the music and for the possibilities yet to be explored. None of the subsidising bodies – record companies, broadcasting authorities, public and private sponsorship – supports jazz to the same extent that they support straight music. Again there would seem to be an ambivalent attitude, that if jazz is now played in the Festival Hall or the Lincoln Centre it should draw enough support to pay for itself – a criterion not applied to a symphony orchestra, nor even a chamber group! There seems to be a refusal to recognise that the contemporary jazz musician is as serious about his art as a straight musician and, unless he's a Dave Brubeck, needs support before worthwhile new work can be done.

REFERENCES

LISTENING

'Blue Rondo à la Turk' on *Dave Brubeck's Greatest Hits* (CBS).
'The Duke' on *Greatest Hits* and on *Miles Ahead* (Evans/Davis).
Jazz Impressions of . . 'Japan' (CBS).
'New York' (CBS).

'Plain Song' on *Jazz Impressions of the USA* (CBS).
Light in the Wilderness (MCA).
Paul Desmond with strings – *Desmond Blue* (RCA). Commercial but beautiful.
Charlie Parker with strings – *The Definitive Charlie Parker*, Volumes 1 and 5 (Metro).
The Mysterious Corona by Palle Mikkelborg on Debut (Denmark). Juxtaposes passages for strings and woodwind quartet with jazz sections.
Focus by Stan Getz with Eddie Sauter (Verve). Particularly 'I'm Late, I'm Late' which joints two alternate takes of the tune where the solo is quite different over the same backing.
Third Stream – 'Silver' (John Lewis with the Orchestra USA), *Anthology*.

FURTHER READING

On subsidy for jazz in Britain – *Inside Jazz*, and *Music Outside* by Carr.

PROJECTS

On jazzing the classics – Is it ever worthwhile? If not why not? If so why? If Maxwell-Davis or Britten can re-work Purcell then why can't Ellington re-work Tchaikovsky? Would Bach have had a rhythm section if he'd been a twentieth-century composer?
On strings in jazz. (Individual musicians have played jazz successfully on violin – Stephan Grappelli and Jean Luc Ponty, but viola has never been used; cello rarely for solos.)
On subsidy for the arts – Should artists starve in a garret?

GENERAL

POINTS TO LISTEN FOR

1. the contrast between the improvising of Brubeck and Desmond
2. the duets between the two
3. Paul Desmond's duets with himself
4. the lack of involvement
5. the artificial use of 'clever' devices.

SUGGESTED RECORDS (best period, the 1960s)

Dave Brubeck's Greatest Hits (CBS). Includes 'Take Five', 'Blue Rondo à la Turk', 'The Duke' and 'Unsquare Dance' (in 7/4).
Jazz Goes to College (CBS).

7 Ornette Coleman

Changes in jazz since the late 1950s

Prior to the emergence of bop in the 1940s, jazz was essentially in 4 beats to a bar, had a regular recurring pulse which was quite definitely stated, used harmonies based on simple diatonically based chord progressions, used material that was based on the blues and standard song form, used theme–solos–theme as the usual structure for development of such forms and, overall, was based on the principle of a soloist with supporting rhythm section.

The bop movement did not, essentially, change these precepts – only alter them. The regular 4/4 pulse stayed, but became less obviously stated and had more complex rhythms superimposed on it. The harmonies stayed as diatonically based progressions but became more complex, vertically by adding extensions to the chords and horizontally by utilising passing chords. The material used was still in the blues and standard song form but the melodic lines were more complex. The general development of the form stayed as theme–solos–theme and, overall, was still strongly soloist based.

Since the late 1950s, though jazz is still played using the pre-bop basics and the bop alterations, jazz musicians have been changing these ideas.

The man generally acknowledged to be most responsible for these changes is Ornette Coleman. One of his earliest champions, John Lewis of The Modern Jazz Quartet, described him as 'an extension of Charlie Parker and one of the first I've heard' but most jazz fans – and many musicians – were critical, and still are in many cases, both of Coleman and the avant garde in general.

Ornette Coleman was born in Fort Worth, Texas in 1930 and he started on tenor saxophone in rhythm and blues bands but later changed to alto. His playing still shows a strong rhythm and blues influence in that it is obviously blues based and strongly rhythmic. He uses the instrument very expressively in his tone, his use of extremes of range – both high, including harmonics, and low, unusual on the alto sax – and in his use of purposely split notes. He creates by these devices and others more *personal* sounds than other well known alto players such as Johnny Hodges, Paul Desmond or even Charlie Parker, and because of this his intonation is sometimes considered odd to well-tempered ears. Unlike Hodges who distorts a note in order to slide into the correct one, Coleman deliberately plays out of tune to give himself additional colour.

Coleman's early years as a musician were difficult. He suffered from being a negro, from being often eccentric in dress and behaviour and for his odd musical ideas. His early records – though they sound fairly conventional to ears attuned to the later excesses of the avant garde – demonstrate the direction in which he was to attack the traditional bases of jazz. The melodies are very angular, though remaining blues based. There is a great interplay between the members of the group and there can be no doubt of the emotion expressed in the playing of Coleman and his trumpeter Don Cherry, an emotionalism which has its roots in early jazz but continues from that expressed by Parker, and is ignored or forgotten by many who followed on from him. His phrases were generally short and seemingly disparate but possessed what Gunther Schuller has referred to as 'a more fragmented, externally disrupted kind of continuity' – and one based on essentially rhythmic and melodic development rather than harmonic. Coleman's credo was 'let's play the music and not the background' meaning that he was dispensing with the customary repetitive chord progressions and replacing it with an intense examination of the rhythmic and melodic possibilities of the tune itself. To quote Schuller again, 'Little motifs are attacked from every conceivable angle, tried sequentially in numerous ways until they yield a motific spring board for a new and contrasting idea, which will in turn be developed similarly, only to yield yet another link in the chain of musical thought, and so on until the entire statement has been made.'

Such analytical understanding of Coleman was rare, though he was, generally, well received by the critics. They were said, by many of the non-believers, to be fearful of being caught napping as almost all the critics were in the furore created by Charlie Parker. And after all, was the assumed reasoning, 'If respected musicians such as John Lewis and Gunther Schuller are raving about Coleman, we had better get on the bandwagon and shout.' While being welcome in some ways – especially for such a difficult music where there are no repetitive chord patterns and there is nothing to follow except the musician's

Ornette Coleman

imagination – it was often overdone. To many critics Coleman was the new Messiah.

Such over-praise did much harm. Coleman's music and that of the other avant garde musicians of the early sixties was not allowed to develop normally but was hothouse fed. It also led to a mistaken over-emphasis of the role Ornette Coleman played in the development of the avant garde. Other musicians such as Miles Davis, John Coltrane, Cecil Taylor and, perhaps surprisingly, Dave Brubeck all contributed. Their efforts often overlapped and resulted in an overhaul of the language of jazz.

REFERENCES

LISTENING

Early Ornette Coleman – *The Shape of Jazz to Come* (Atlantic).
  Change of the Century (Atlantic).
  The Art of the Improvisers (Atlantic).

FURTHER READING

On Coleman and Cecil Taylor – *Four Lives in the Bebop Business* by A. B. Spellman (Macgibbon & Kee, 1967).

PROJECT

On criticism – Do critics have a place – and what is it? Can they influence an art or a specific artist? Should musicians take note of critics? Should the listener take note of criticism?

Coleman's influence

The interplay between the group members shown in Coleman's records led to a gradual breakdown of the barriers between soloist and rhythm section. Since bop there had been an increasing trend away from the dance-based, and therefore heavily stated, rhythms of the swing era. Because the music was no longer functional there was no need for the beat to be stated so strongly – or indeed even stated at all. If a pulse *was* used, it was most often used in new ways. Coleman used a pulse but did not divide it into bar lengths by accenting or implying an accent on the first beat of every four. Often the music does fall into this pattern but this happens by chance rather than design. The music flows over a basic pulse with the accents falling freely rather than in accordance with some predetermined pattern. Other groups moved away from a dependence on a pulse at all, creating patterns of sound with no rhythmic base. Others still moved away from the 4/4 pulse but utilised new time signatures. 3/4 had been in use in jazz for some time as had 6/4 or 6/8 but Dave Brubeck was responsible for using 5, 7, 9 and even 11 beat patterns and though the results were often wooden, placing too much dependence on the pattern rather than the melody and the improvising, he certainly established that it could be done and opened the way for many others.

Harmonies have been altered in three basic ways: the simplification of them established by Miles Davis in his modal experiments in *Kind of Blue* and the continuation of these ideas, albeit in a different way, by John Coltrane; the move away from diatonically based cycle of 5ths chord progressions; and Coleman's complete disregard for any harmony except that accidentally caused by simultaneous lines.

As harmonies and rhythms have got freer so have themes. There is no longer the dependence on the basic forms of the blues and standard song. Melodic lines are sketchier, often, as with rhythm, making their point by implication rather than by direct statement. They are also often more angular and use a higher degree of dissonance than before.

The development of these melodies is often freer also, being based on a continuance of the mood, rather than a repetition of the form. The days of the dominating soloist have also passed, first with the elevation of the rhythm section to equal status and then with the return to collective improvisation which has developed in the new jazz. The problems of intensity – of the sheer raw unrelenting power which was prevalent in the early days is, fortunately, solving itself, as groups and musicians realise that the music has to breathe, that there must be some ebb and flow and that loud passages mean more when contrasted with soft.

This last point, and indeed all the attacks on tradition, alienated fans of the bop period and before but perhaps the biggest factor in the misunderstanding and plain dislike of the avant garde is the new vocabulary of sounds. As Coleman shows the alto sax is capable of being much more expressive in sound quality than even Parker demonstrated. By use of distorted intonation and sounds from his rhythm and blues days on tenor he has a complete vocabulary of honks, growls, smears, squeaks, glisses and other noises. He also took up violin and trumpet but, as A. B. Spellman says in his essay on

Ornette Coleman in *Four Lives in the Bebop Business*, 'he was not interested in playing Bach partitas; he was interested in playing Ornette Coleman'.

Other musicians also have expanded the sound possibilities on their instruments: saxophonists have extended the upper range; pianists such as Cecil Taylor use dissonant clusters for their noise components rather than to establish a harmony, and they treat the piano primarily as a percussion instrument; drummers have incorporated a whole battery of new instruments, or sound producers, into their equipment; trombonists have reintroduced glissandi and smears. By the use of such sounds avant garde musicians often show an intensity of expression which is considered ugly or disturbing, but such sounds developed from a reaction against the clinical similarities of sound of the bop players. Almost all alto saxophone players tried to sound like Parker, all trombonists like J. J. Johnson, and so on. These sounds are an attempt to re-widen the vocabulary of jazz: a return, in an indirect way, to the vocal mannerisms and raw emotions of earlier jazz.

Listening to avant garde

Because of these noise elements in the avant garde there is a tendency to believe that the musicians involved are bluffing, that they cannot really play. There is also the parallel drawn that proof of musicianship entails being able to play a solo on, say, the chords of 'How High the Moon'. If they can do that then their avant garde music may not become more acceptable but at least there is proof 'that he can play jazz' and that they 'are not faking all the time'. This is unfair; perhaps a musician would be a better player if he could solo on 'How High the Moon', all experience is useful, but it is not *necessary* for him to do so to prove his worth.

The only criterion for judging an avant garde musician is communication: whether his language, or rather his accent in the language of avant garde jazz, is acceptable to you and communicates to you. Unfortunately though, such communicative moments are often lost in a morass of less happy ones, a problem with all jazz but one more apparent – and more possible because of its generally more questing status – in the avant garde. A major criticism of the avant garde is that if chords, pulse and theme are dispensed with, it will all sound the same. The short answer is that a lot of it does but the musicians are now learning that there are immense responsibilities and demands associated with these freedoms; they must listen *all* the time; there is no 'coasting by' playing old clichés on well-known chord patterns, and they must create music by *interaction*: very difficult and rarely achieved but not to be ignored because of that.

The present avant garde seems to have split into two main streams, the American and the European. The European is more cerebral, bearing close affinities to straight avant garde, and in fact many musicians work in both areas with equal fluency. The American stream, which was known for a while as Black Music (though white Americans such as Roswell Rudd, and even non-Americans like Argentinian saxophone player Gato Barbieri, were involved in it), is much more jazz orientated and the sounds produced are generally warmer and more personal.

It should be remembered, however, that there are many facets of contemporary jazz apart from the extreme playing which is classified as avant garde. Some follow on from Miles Davis's modal experiments – either composing directly from scales or extracting a scale for solos from a previously composed melody. Others continue using time playing and chord sequences but look at both in a new manner. The time is played much looser, the chords have moved away from variations of the cycle of 5ths approach which dominated jazz for so many years. All would have developed along similar lines without the avant garde but they would not have been as rich in colour and ideas if the avant garde had not existed.

Many people believe that, both in America and Europe, the avant garde – and indeed all contemporary jazz – has gone as far as it ever will, that from now on musicians are destined simply to explore the same directions. It may be that they are right and that the legacy of the avant garde is that it has forced a re-examination of old traditions and that it has returned to jazz some of its old tone colours as well as introducing some new ones. At present we are too close to see, but at least it has restored to jazz an emotion and intensity necessary to it but so often sadly lacking.

REFERENCES

LISTENING

Later Coleman – 'Chappaqua Suite' (1965), *Anthology*.
Some recommended avant garde records –

Archie Shepp – *Mama Too Tight* (Impulse).
Cecil Taylor – *Nuits de la Foundation Maeght*, Volumes 1 and 2 (Shandar, France).
Charles Mingus – *Charles Mingus* (Prestige).
Gato Barbieri and Roswell Rudd on *Escalator Over the Hill* (JCOA Records) by Carla Bley.
London Jazz Composer's Orchestra – *Ode* (Incus). Includes most British avant garde musicians.

PROJECTS

A study of the sounds used in jazz, possibly by a comparison between them and the sounds of straight music.
A study of the way the piano has developed in jazz (possibly using the tracks on the *Anthology*).
Ditto with the drums.
Ditto with the rhythm section as a whole.
On the avant garde in other arts. Do they really reflect our time as many people seem to think?

GENERAL

POINTS TO LISTEN FOR

(NB This music could be considered difficult to listen to as there is no harmonic base. One must listen freely without previous conceptions as to what one believes jazz to be.)
1. the rhythmic and melodic stress of the improvisations
2. the additional vocabulary of sounds
3. the interactions between members of the group in their exchange of *ideas* (particularly between the drums and the soloist)
4. the dynamic range and sounds of the drums (particularly Charlie Moffatt).

SUGGESTED RECORDS (no best period)

Golden Circle, Volume 1 (Blue Note). Particularly Dee Dee.
The Shape of Jazz to Come (Atlantic).
The Best of Ornette Coleman (Atlantic).

FURTHER READING

Essay on Coleman in *Four Lives in the Bebop Business* by A. B. Spellman (Macgibbon & Kee, 1967).

PART TWO

8 The teaching of jazz

Before a student tries to play jazz he must have some command over his instrument – even if he only wants to play avant garde jazz, and that is not as flippant as it might seem. Some time ago I heard a jazz course organiser say 'We have to look after those who can't play yet so we'll have to teach them to play avant garde!'

Ideally he should also have had some experience in creative music – some experience in making sounds in company with others. And that, basically, is all jazz is. There is most often some sort of regular pulse (implied if not stated) and some rhythmic syncopation against that pulse; the sounds produced are often coloured by various distortions of the tone but, basically, jazz like all improvised music is just personal creation.

Such personal creation is best done in small groups where everyone has a chance to be heard without chaos developing. Ideally such groups should have some soloists (between one and four) and a rhythm section of piano, bass and drums. Adaptations can be made and where possible they are mentioned in the text. It is difficult to put a larger group of musicians into an improvising situation, as essentially jazz is a kind of chamber music dependent on interaction between musicians. Again, though, suggestions are made where possible.

One well-tried way is the conventional big band, stage band or dance band with 4 or 5 trumpets, 3, 4, or 5 trombones, 4 or 5 saxes and piano, bass, drums and, possibly, guitar. Administratively this is easy to organise in that 15–20 people are under the control of one teacher and material, of a kind, is readily available. It teaches disciplines like playing in a section *as* a section and solving the resultant phrasing and intonation problems. But *individuality*, the very thing that jazz should be teaching, is usually stifled. The majority of arrangements available come from what I call the predictable area of big band writing and have scope for individuality only in the solo sections – a very exposed area for the young player where he is thrown into the deep end of improvising on a sink-or-swim basis; most young players are not ready for such exposure. The big band needs to be part of any education programme but it needs better material where more involvement is expected. There is also the need for a repertoire of good standard material arranged by such people as Ellington, Gil Evans and Gerry Mulligan. There is a feel about playing in an Ellington-type saxophone section where each note has its distinctive place that should be a part of every jazz musician's make-up. Sadly though what is often offered is ersatz Woody Herman or 'Lil Darling'. A thrill to play once in a while perhaps but not at all helpful (after the first few times) in an educational sense – where the aim should be to develop the creativity of the musicians.

Formal education in jazz

There are two opposing views of formal education in jazz – both expressed in comments by Duke Ellington. The first, when asked for his advice on whether one of his musicians should study at music college, was 'you'll only learn what you already know . . . and it will mess you up'; the second was the comment made to pianist Cecil Taylor, 'you need the conservatory, with an ear for what's happening on the streets'. Both points of view have truth in them but the fact that they were made more than twenty years apart is indicative of a change in the music and in attitudes to education.

At the time of Ellington's first answer (around 1940) the school in question – Juilliard – had a reputation for being an advanced school, but not one specialising in jazz, and in fact there were at that time no specialised jazz courses. Naturally all music colleges will teach the basics of musicianship but these will obviously be slanted towards the college's main function – the turning out of good orchestral players and soloists – and not to the particular needs of a jazz musician. As Ellington implied, the man in his band *knew* how to play his instrument and formal training would perhaps have stifled his individuality.

By the time of the second statement jazz had changed. Opportunities for self education were lessening; there were increasing technical demands on the players and there was a growing awareness of the peculiar needs of jazz in an educational situation. As Ellington pointed out though, even with a conservatory education you need 'an ear for what's happening on the streets' – you need to be aware of the world around you and aware that education is a continuing process, that you ultimately educate yourself.

The process of complete self education was of course a necessity in jazz until fairly recently. Musicians learnt to improvise by listening to others, Charlie Parker learning Lester Young solos by heart, Miles Davis leaving Juilliard because he was learning more listening to Parker. They also learnt by playing with others either in jam sessions (after-hours sessions where musicians got together to improvise – sometimes resulting in cutting competitions to see who was best), or in travelling bands.

Such bands also provided a cruel but necessary reminder of the jazz musicians' separation from other creative arts. They can, because they are singular arts, be done when the artist wishes; jazz because it is a co-operative art and one linked to an entertainment situation must be done to order, and though jazz musicians are generally keen to play, there are inevitably times when the desire has gone. They also provide a training in playing in constantly changing situations – in large hall or small club, in recording studio or television studio.

Composers too learnt by trial and error. Duke Ellington, while working at the Cotton Club in Harlem, had to provide scores for the exotic production number in the nightly cabaret and it was this that gave him the opportunity to explore the possibilities of sound within the band, a process of exploration which his contemporaries, who provided music solely for dancing, had no need to do. He can be heard on recordings of that period trying the same ideas on several different pieces till he knew that it worked and why it worked.

This of course is still a possible way of learning to write but there is much less opportunity nowadays for practical experience either in cabarets or travelling bands, and a good jazz education provides, in more contemporary form, a replacement for these. My own training, at the Berklee School of Music in Boston, gave me the opportunity to work with all sorts of bands in all sorts of situations; the wholesale production of big band scores in a more or less conventional style has left me reasonably fluent in that idiom and I felt able to move on to more adventurous use of the medium. I could have attained this away from Berklee but there is no doubt it would have taken much longer. On a very practical level musicians to play the arrangements were always available there; elsewhere they would be much more difficult – if not impossible – to gather together.

The main advantage of such colleges is the opportunity they give one of learning from the experience of others. This stimulates the student's mind to examine each point constructively and to explore new aspects. For example certain notes can be added to a C major chord which will thicken the chord but not affect its tonality.

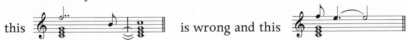

Other notes will raise problems but there is no reason why *any* note should not be used in improvising or arranging on a C major chord without its tonality being altered. It's a matter of how it's used, and a teacher can say

this  is wrong and this

is allowable. In between the student must establish things for himself.

Of course this learning from the experience of others need not necessarily involve teachers. An aware student learns by observing at close hand the way others deal with a situation and he establishes his own methods. This interaction between students is also vitally important in good jazz education (if not in *all* education).

Practical suggestions are given later for sparking off such inter-action and for stimulating awareness in students.

9 Improvisation

How do you improvise? What makes jazz improvising different from the improvising in Indian music or aleatoric music? How do you learn to improvise?

These are the sort of questions that a jazz musician is asked. His answers are often vague and terse – 'Well I just blow' – and the fact is that often this is as much as he knows. He may say he plays around the tune, or takes the chord sequence and tries to build a new melody on it, or thinks of a motif and tries to make it fit over all the chords he is playing, but basically he's just playing.

There is an analogy here with walking. If you are asked 'How do you walk?' the answer might be, 'Well . . . I just put one leg in front of the other, shift the weight on to the front leg, and so on ad infinitum'; the same when a jazz musician improvises – he just puts down his valves or key and blows. But if we were to walk without being aware (usually unconsciously) of the 'supporting structure' (the pavement) and the hazards (kerbs, traffic, other pedestrians) then we would stumble and possibly fall flat on our face. Similarly in improvising, if we are not aware of the supporting structure – the harmony, melody, rhythm and mood of the piece – then we shall stumble by playing a wrong note, and if we play too many wrong notes we shall meta-phorically fall flat on our face. There are also, when walking, *potential* hazards like a broken piece of pavement we have to cross each day and *unexpected* hazards like suddenly turning traffic, wayward dogs on leashes. These again have their analogy in improvising – the potential hazard of a strange chord or a change of tempo, the unexpected hazard of a drum fill on the wrong beat or a weird voicing by the pianist. As an improviser you have to learn how to deal with the potential hazard and how to negate the effect of the unexpected. Ideally the improviser should be so sure of himself that he *never* stumbles – and that, to return for a final time to our walking analogy, is very rare.

A jazz musician though is sometimes more articulate about his improvising and can give some clues to his method, though these rarely give the full answer.

If an improviser says he 'plays around the melody', what does he do? To take a simple motif

he may change it slightly, say into

where he alters the value of the notes

or

where he leaves notes out or he could alter it more drastically but still retain the flavour of the melody

But why he chose those particular rhythm and notes in preference to all the other possibilities remains a mystery.

If he favours making a new melody he could improvise, over the F7 chord

or, if he were more adventurous

or, to be more adventurous still

If he wants he can explore a motif more fully by placing it over each new chord and altering it rhythmically and melodically as he does so. This is illustrated here using the last motif over a basic blues sequence.

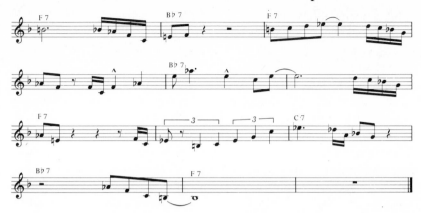

Here the elements the soloist has stressed are the dissonance and the four short descending notes. The dissonance (or a similar one) appears in bars 1, 2, 3, 5, 6, 7 (on the second quaver), 8 (on the second note), 9 and 11. The four short notes appear in bars 1, 3, 6 and, expanded, in bar 10. All these elements, even though they may not be immediately apparent to the listener, and were not consciously thought of by the soloist, give the solo some inner continuity: it hangs together as a piece of music.

The dictionary definition of improvisation is of very little help, stating as it does 'to compose or perform without preparation'. But of course, without being pedantic, there is always preparation. First the potential jazz improviser must practise his instrument till he is technically competent. It is not necessary that he be able to play everything on his instrument but it is necessary that he know what he can play. Miles Davis, in his early years with Charlie Parker, lacked range and a fast technique but he created good solos by playing *within* his technique, by not trying to play something on almost every chord as Parker did but by cutting his coat to fit his cloth. There is preparation also in the fact that the soloist has probably played the piece before, or seen something similar, and is therefore slightly prepared for some of the problems he will face. As part of his training a soloist will have practised playing between difficult chords or changing tempo suddenly and if he is caught out in a piece by something strange he will try to remember the problem – and how he solved it – in order that he won't get caught again. He may have played on a set of chords so often that his fingers lead him into clichéd patterns and his whole solo is, subconsciously, prepared although any good player is on his guard against this. He may if he is lazy – or easily satisfied – have come to accept one solution as the only one he thinks of when faced with a certain situation. Then there is Duke Ellington's point 'Sure all improvising is thought out beforehand, though some is only thought out a split second before . . .'

Listening to jazz improvising will start to give an idea of what it means but only in a limited way. One can tell when listening to Charlie Parker that he is playing around the extensions of the chords, but not all the time; that Thelonious Monk will repeat a fragment of melody in a new way almost through an entire solo (but what about the times he doesn't?); that Coleman Hawkins was a much simpler player than Parker, Coltrane much more complex than Davis, but *what are they doing*? They are not just playing anything; there is a difference when Parker stops one tune and starts another – even in two versions of the same tune there is a marked difference. It is not just playing variations on the melody either. Though many musicians do use elements of the theme when improvising, others regard it merely as a provider of the chord sequence or, in more contemporary jazz, as the provider of the mood.

This last point brings the problem of defining jazz improvisation into sharper focus as it divorces jazz from its previous tradition of being always associated with chords and a regular pulse.

The jazz improviser derives his ideas from the basic elements (melody, harmony, rhythm) in the framework he is given, plus the additional one of mood. Some soloists concentrate more on one than the other; some kinds of framework stress one more than the other; some frameworks exclude one (or more) of these elements; but these are the basics and it is how the soloist uses them – how his use of them appeals to you as a listener – that makes him into a good soloist or not.

Louis Armstrong came from a tradition of collective improvisation – each instrument with a prescribed role, the trumpet's to play the melody, the others' to improvise within their own roles around the chords. As jazz moved away from collective improvisation to solo statements, a mixture of the two became the norm.

The development of improvisation

During the swing era soloists concentrated more on chords. The melody was acknowledged occasionally but the soloist built his improvisation by using the notes of the chords to create his own melodies.

Bebop took this further in that melodies were mostly used as 'launching pads' only. The chord sequence reigned supreme and it didn't seem to matter what tune they played as long as the chords were good to play on. Harmonies were extended both by adding chords to the sequence and by the soloist using, in his improvisation, the upper parts of the chords. Set against that were the melodic improvisations of Thelonious Monk and Sonny Rollins. Monk comes closest to the theme and variations approach in jazz, believing that whatever the melody is it should feature strongly in his solos. Rollins is more subtle, thinking up his own melodic motif and then worrying it around, looking at it from all angles.

By the fifties harmonies had reached their ultimate in complexity and reaction set in. On the one hand Ornette Coleman ignored harmony as such, concentrating on melody and rhythm, producing a style with echoes of early blues in its use of vocalised sounds but with a complexity of rhythms laid against the basic pulse. On the other hand Miles Davis simplified chord structures, concentrating on improvising on a scale rather than a chord progression. He prophesied that a movement was beginning in jazz 'away from the conventional string of chords, and a return to emphasis on melodic rather than harmonic variation. There will be fewer chords but infinite possibilities as to what to do with them.' Two of the possibilities were dramatically shown in Davis's own approach to scales, and John Coltrane's. Davis simplified matters, leaving one note to carry over several bars, perhaps; Coltrane, reasoning that scales can only differ in a few notes, decided to try to get every note in on every chord and produced his aptly named 'sheets of sound' approach.

In all of these styles there is the additional consideration of mood – the mood of the original song and the mood of its development by the player. In recent years, though, mood has predominated, at times doing away completely with any preconceived melody, harmony and rhythm. Musicians improvise together *completely* spontaneously, having no preconceived framework at all, dependent on the other musicians to stimulate their ideas. Sometimes a tune with or without harmonies will be used to set up the mood, but once it is played the soloists take no further notice of its structure or harmonies, working either from a scale, usually derived from the melody, or completely freely.

All these styles of improvising co-exist in jazz and perhaps the only thing that separates them from other kinds of improvising is the personal approach of the player. If we compare some straight improvising with jazz we find that in the former the improviser is generally subordinate to the composer. He usually works within clearly defined limits and his range of sounds is much cleaner, more impersonal than those of the jazz musician. The *sounds* of an aleatoric piece played by a group in New York will be essentially the same as those made by a group playing the same piece in London, though the result may be different. The sounds of a free jazz piece, and the results, will be completely different in any two groups. Improvising jazz musicians have a wider range of personal sounds than their straight counterparts. But, to complicate matters, many players now work in both the straight and jazz avant gardes.

Contemporary rock improvising is heavily jazz influenced but is usually less subtle in content and in the basic pulse. *Personality* can be expressed more in jazz improvising also.

A comparison with the improvising in Indian music shows there are many similarities: both improvise on a rhythmic pulse, both use a framework of scale and mood. Also of course Indian improvising is personal; there is enough freedom in the music and enough strength in the great players for them to impress their mark on a piece. The only difference is that jazz improvisers use the Afro-American heritage of the music, in particular its vocalised sounds and blues notes, and Indian improvisers use their own heritage of micro-tones etc.

There seems to be very little difference then and it may not be too far-fetched to broaden our definition of jazz to include Indian music. Ravi Shankar and Ali Akbar Khan could be said to be great jazz musicians: they improvise in a very personal way on a rhythmic base, and only the accent is different. As mentioned earlier, Gunther Schuller is investigating a possible connection between the blues and Indian music.

There would seem to be only one connecting link between all the different styles of improvising in jazz. It is not, as many people may imagine, the pulse or the chord progression; jazz improvising can exist without either. It is that all are expressions of the player's individuality and that, simply, is what jazz is or should be about. The definition can be qualified by saying that improvisation is generally over a steady pulse, often uses a chord progression, almost always uses vocalised, highly personal sounds, but not always, and it is always an individual expression. It is spontaneous but each note should seem inevitable and right, and there should always be a sense of surprise. As critic Charles Fox said 'the unexpected suddenly becomes transformed into the inevitable'.

Any reaction to jazz – as any art – must be subjective. There are no hard and fast rules of right and wrong, all that counts is the musician's honesty. He states his individual message which hopefully communicates to others.

REFERENCES

LISTENING

Examples of many of the great improvisers in jazz can be heard on the *Anthology*. These include Louis Armstrong, Bix Beiderbecke, Coleman Hawkins, Lester Young, Charlie Christian, Dizzy Gillespie, Miles Davis and John Coltrane.

Comparisons can be made between, say, all the pianists, or between the styles of the major figures like Louis Armstrong, Lester Young, Miles Davis and Ornette Coleman. (There is, unfortunately, no Charlie Parker on the *Anthology*.)

FURTHER READING

Improvising Jazz by Jerry Coker (Prentice Hall paperback).
Jazz Improvisation by Dave Baker (Maher, 1969).
Jazz Improvisation by John Mehagan (2 volumes, Watson-Guptill Publications). Volume II contains comparisons of twelve major soloists on the blues including Armstrong, Young and Parker.
A New Approach to Jazz Improvisation by Jamie Abersold. Two guide books and two records.
The Lydian Chromatic Concept of Tonal Organisation (for improvisation) by George Russell (Concept Publications NY, 1959).
There is some discussion of improvisation and the individual approach of different jazz musicians on the Lecture Concert Record.

The teaching of improvisation

Most jazz musicians seem to have learnt to improvise by a combination of basic interest, encouraged by listening to records and live jazz; inherent ability, amplified by practising for technical command, and playing with the right people at the right time. A teacher can help by showing what to listen for and how to apply it (in other situations), and by showing the right things to practise to develop certain necessary skills. These practice techniques, if refined down to basics, can be of great assistance to young musicians taking their first steps in jazz improvising.

PRACTICAL

Basic improvising

Jazz improvising is most often done over a regular pulse and the concept of rhythm in a jazz sense comes from the subtle accents on the basic pulse and the syncopations over it.

The first exercises deal with improvising from a given motif over such a regular pulse. (At this stage there are no harmonies intended other than those set up by the motif itself, therefore the pulse should be tapped rather than played.)

First establish a regular pulse by tapping x x x x x x x x x x x etc., and subdivide it into four by making a subtle accent on the first of every four *x* x x x *x* x x x *x* x x x etc.

Then take a simple phrase such as

and play it over the pulse, trying to vary it by altering it *rhythmically* only.

These can be un-syncopated

syncopated

and can include rests

Syncopation

This is a change of emphasis on a normally unaccented beat. In jazz this is usually achieved by anticipating the 1st and 3rd beats by a quaver ($\frac{1}{8}$th note, ♪) but any beat may be syncopated and rhythms such as

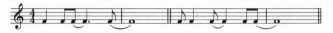

are common.

If any trouble is found reading syncopations they are best sub-divided into 8 (e.g. into 8 quavers when in 4/4). Jazz quavers are not played exactly but are given almost a ♩ ♪ feel. In other words

is not played exactly but more like

(Listening to any jazz musician will show the correct way.) See Chapter 12, 'Arranging', for notes on the writing of quavers.

This type of exercise can be done with two or more soloists either trying to copy each other or else trying to follow on and develop the other's ideas. They can also be repeated using motifs thought up by one of the players and at varying tempos. Attention should also be paid to changing dynamics and octaves to create further interest. Be careful not to over-use such exercises as a good player can get a lot from them but a not-so-good player may become frustrated and bored.

Illustrations Record track 1 commences with a tapped pulse, sub-divided into 4 beats to a bar. The first soloist uses the notes of the motif above to create a solo. This is followed by a duet on the notes of the motif and, finally, a duet on the motif plus added notes. The intention was to make the solo musically interesting and still retain the *flavour* of the motif. Such motifs should always be regarded as the point of departure for an individual statement, however limited that statement may be at first.

Addition of notes

These can be added:
before the basic motif

after the basic motif

inside the basic motif

The notes can be added from a specific tonality as in the above examples or at random. These exercises played by two or more players can be an excellent way of training the ear. Again, they should be repeated using new motifs.

Transposition

This can be a useful way of varying the interest of a simple motif. It can be done by exact transposition

by transposing within the key

or by contour transposition (following the general shape)

This can include the alteration of the original motif by use of accidentals

(A listing of transformation techniques is given in Appendix VIII.)

At this stage the student should have a vocabulary of rhythmic and melodic techniques, plus the use of dynamics, by which he can alter the initial motif while still leaving it very recognisable.

Using harmony

As well as just tapping, the basic pulse can suggest a tonality or harmony by having a single repeated note or two or more notes in a pattern played by a piano, bass or chime bars etc.

Illustrations Record track 2 has one soloist building an improvisation from the motif using all the techniques so far available, first on pedal C then a pattern suggesting C minor.

Group exercises can be attempted as follows:
   1. making up a repeating bass pattern

   2. making up a basic motif to fit over the bass pattern

   3. writing the motif in four different rhythms

and establishing a form such as
4 bars of pattern (which continues throughout)
4 bars of the motif played in rhythm (1)
4 bars of a soloist improvising on the motif
4 bars of the motif played in rhythm (2)
4 bars of a new soloist improvising on the motif
repeating in a similar way for as long as required.

Illustrations Record track 3 has the band playing in such a way on the motifs above. (Note each soloist's different approach to the motif.)

Appendix I deals with chord types and nomenclature. Appendix V discusses the use of the guitar, piano, bass and drums as a rhythm section if they are available. The composition *Darius* on the Lecture Concert Record, contains much motific improvisation. It is analysed in the accompanying booklet.

10 The blues

The dictionary defines blues as 'a slow dismal type of song' but it is much more than that to a jazz musician. Essentially the blues is an atmosphere, an indefinable something that permeates jazz and which Charles Fox describes as 'a climate of feeling'. It is also a form – a sequence of chords – much used in jazz and pop music, and it is used as a generic term for a folk music outside jazz but closely linked to it, and one of the seeds from which jazz grew.

The beginning of the blues was vocal. The negro slaves brought into America were encouraged to sing by their owners to make them work better. Naturally these 'hollers' and 'field songs' expressed their African origins and it is interesting to note that a similar *feeling* to that of the blues can be seen in the hondo style of the Spanish folk singers and the fado singing of Portugal, both with origins in slave movements. There is also the theory, already mentioned, that the blues arrived in the Southern United States after travelling from India into Europe and Africa through the Arab world. This too would link the blues-like music of Spain and Portugal with American blues.

The first blues singers in America were wandering negro minstrels, sometimes blind. They travelled from town to town making a living by singing the blues and accompanying themselves on the guitar. This 'country blues' enjoyed a revival in England in the 1960s through visits by bluesmen like Big Bill Broonzy and Muddy Waters and started a rhythm and blues boom which led, via the Beatles and the Rolling Stones, to a resurgence of interest in the blues in America.

The lyrics of such singers were very personal – most often songs of trouble: poverty, drink, sex or natural disasters – but they could be more exuberant, often with a sly wit. The form is simply 3 lines, with the first being repeated and a concluding phrase for line 3. After each line the singer would usually improvise a fill-in phrase on his guitar before moving on to the next.

This approach became prominent in the classic blues period when singers, most often female, sang the blues as part of the entertainment of the time. They were often accompanied by jazz musicians such as Louis Armstrong, improvising behind the singer and between the phrases.

The original country blues singers were very loose with the form. They used 3 phrases but often varied their length. Once the blues became established as an instrumental form in early New Orleans jazz, a 12-bar structure, 3 phrases of 4 bars, became the norm. 8- and 16-bar blues are known and in fact some of the more famous early blues, perhaps showing the influence of the more complex structures common in ragtime, are more complicated. *St Louis Blues* for example is 12 12 16 bars and *Beale Street Blues* is 12 12 8. Some contemporary musicians have returned to the original looseness of country blues and play blues with an odd number of bars. Remember though, that not all pieces called '. . . Blues' are in fact in the accepted blues structure.

The harmonic base of the blues evolved from the hymns sung by the slaves, and using the three basic chords of tonic, subdominant and dominant. The basic harmonic scheme in C would be

1	2	3	4
C	C	C	C or C7

5	6	7	8
F	F	C	C

9	10	11	12
G7	G7	C	C

It seems capable of infinite variation without losing its character. Three possibilities would be

1.
C	F	C	C7
F	F—	E — 7	C
G7	F	C F	C

2.
C	F7 B♭7	A7 D7	G — 7 C7
F	F—	E — 7	A7
D — 7	G7	C B♭7	C
		or C A7	D — 7 G7

3.
C69	F — 7	E — 7 D — 7	C♯ — 7 F♯7
F	F — 7 B♭7	E — 7 A7	E♭ — 7 A♭7
D — 7	A♭ — 6	E — 7 E♭ — 7	D — 7 G7
(G in bass)			

The latter is typical of a blues in the bop era but contemporary jazz – following on from Miles Davis's experiments with modes – has often returned to the very basic chord sequence, outlined sometimes by a repetitive bass pattern.

Improvising on the blues

The blues sequence has been a fertile source of material for the jazz composer. The classic blues form is a 2-bar melody, often a variation on a chordal arpeggio, followed by a 2-bar gap for an improvised fill; transposition of that melody up a 4th to accommodate the new chord; further transposition or a new melody in bars 9 and 10 to finish it off (this form follows the lyric form mentioned earlier).

Sometimes the melody could be played over the transposed chord without alteration – or with only one note or so altered – and such a superimposition often became the basis of swing era blues compositions, many of which were 'head' arrangements, made up on the spot.

Bebop blues were sometimes riff orientated but often much more complex, sounding like written out improvisations which they perhaps were. John Carisi's 'Israel', written for the Miles Davis *Birth of the Cool* session is much more, though, and ranks as a great miniature composition. Even the chord sequence shows signs of great care.

The climate of feeling is, as was said, indefinable though it derives from the vocal traditions of jazz and the individual touches of jazz improvisers. These include the catalogue of growls, smears, glisses, and shakes as well as the more subtle use of personal tone and vibrato. There are the 'blue notes' too, the ♭3, ♭7 and sometimes ♭5 used in a major key to capture the effect of the early blues singers who sang in a non-tempered scale. In the blues motif used earlier in the chapter

there is a blue 3rd, giving the melody its particular character. Without these alterations the melody would be very colourless.

To accommodate these blue notes the basic chord structure is often altered to a series of dominant type chords where the blue 3rd is thought of as a raised 9th (the symbol means repeat the chord).

C7	⁄.	⁄.	⁄.
F7	⁄.	C7	⁄.
G7	⁄.	C7	⁄.

REFERENCES

LISTENING

Louis Armstrong and Bessie Smith – 'St Louis Blues', *Anthology*. NB The form is two blues choruses plus 16 bars.
Billie Holiday – 'Mean to Me', *Anthology*. Not a blues.
Archie Shepp – 'Mama Too Tight' (13-bar blues), *Mama Too Tight* (Impulse).
Other examples of blues from the *Anthology* include:

'West End Blues' – Louis Armstrong.
'St Louis Blues' – Art Tatum (piano solo). See note above.
'Blues' – Jimmy Blanton and Duke Ellington (bass and piano duet).
'Waltz Limps' – Dave Brubeck (blues in 3/4).

PRACTICAL

The basic blues chord progression can provide the basis for much
improvising practice.

It can be suggested by simple rhythmic patterns such as

which are transposed to fit the changes of chord in bars 5 and 9. (See
the first music example in this chapter.)

These patterns can be played on piano, bass, chime bars etc., or if a
rhythm section is available they can elaborate on the basic patterns by
using some of the ideas suggested in Appendix V.

This type of pattern can be used to familiarise *all* the players with
the chord movements within a blues sequence.

again transposing them in bars 5 and 9.

Also the students can play sustained chords, changing when the
chord changes. At first perhaps by designating notes of the chord,
'you play the root each time, you the third' etc.; then later by allowing
them to choose which note of the basic chord they will play (possibly
nominating one for the root) thus creating new, albeit simple, textures
each time. Various note values can be used from tied semibreves to
crotchets, or various rhythm patterns

Then various melodies can be applied to these rhythms at first using just chord notes.

(Any other instruments should double the melody where it is written or an octave beneath.)

A dominant 7th blues progression can also be used in this way

(Transpositions for the changes of chord should, if at all possible, be made by the student to familiarise them thoroughly with chords.)

Once complete familiarity has been gained with the blue sequence improvising can be tried using a motif as in the previous chapter.

Illustrations Record track 4 has one soloist improvising over a basic blues sequence using one of the earlier motifs.

Improvising can also be tried direct from the chords, either alone

or by adding passing notes to each chord

Illustrations Record track 5 starts with this idea and continues with chordal improvising – with passing notes – over a basic blues sequence.

The remainder of the group can be playing sustained backgrounds or riffs (either pre-arranged or possibly improvised by one and picked up by the others). Such riffs could be played in bars 1 and 2 of the blues and answered by an improvised fill from one of the soloists.

NB Blue notes should wherever possible be used in such backings and of course solos, but they should be used *naturally*.

Illustrations Record track 6 shows this approach.

Tape track 1: blues in F with simple chords and simple rhythm section playing; *track 2:* blues in F with more complex chords and rhythm section playing; *track 3:* slow blues in F (12/8 feel); *track 4:* fast blues in F.

Further exercises

The blues should be practised in various keys, either alone or in a group situation. This can be done by transposing successive choruses around a cycle – either 5ths, 4ths, 3rd, minor 3rd, 2nds or semitones.

Tape track 5 has one chorus of the blues in every key. (Going around the cycle of 5ths starting on C, then F, then B♭ and so on. Each key is named at the start.)

Soloists can take solos in turns every chorus, every 4 bars, every 8 bars etc.

More complex chord progressions can be used. There are some examples earlier in this chapter and Appendix III gives some hints for altering chord progressions.

The group can play a riff in the first 4 bars of every chorus and soloists can follow (a new one each time) to finish off the chorus.

NB Always stress the necessity for space. The improvisation must have room to breathe.

11 The popular song form

The popular song, like the blues, has been a fertile source of raw material for the jazz musician. Jazz improvisers have offered versions of popular material from the trite, like 'Hello, Dolly', to the sublime, like 'Body and Soul'. Jazz composers have written new melodies over existing chord sequences, like Charlie Parker's 'Ornithology' over the chords of 'How High the Moon', or composed completely new melodies using the popular song form, 'So What' or 'Round about Midnight' for example.

Unfortunately the standard song is nowhere near as easy to discuss as the blues. There is no one basic form; no one basic chord progression; no basic melodic patterns. Songs do, however, have certain things in common.

Form

Usually 32 bars in length (8 8 8 8).

Often only two main themes — possibly with slight variations — organised as AABA, with A as the first 8-bar theme, B as the second.

AABA songs are 'Smoke Gets in Your Eyes', 'September in the Rain', 'Polka Dots and Moonbeams', 'Body and Soul'.

Another popular form is ABAC: 'Stardust' and 'Embraceable You'.

Chords

The chord sequence follows the form of the melody (i.e. a repeated theme will have the same chords on each repeat) and is usually diatonically based. The chords of George Gershwin's 'I Got Rhythm' (AABA form) are:

A section

1	2	3	4
B♭ G−7	C−7 F7	B♭ G−7	C−7 F7
5	6	7	8
B♭ B♭7	E♭ E♭−	B♭ F7	B♭

B section

17	18	19	20
D7	˙/.	G7	˙/.
21	22	23	24
C7	˙/.	F7	˙/.

There is a marked change of approach in the chords of the B section (known as the bridge, the *middle* 8 or the release).

The dominant 7ths resolve, round the cycle of 5ths, back to the home key. Other tunes though do actually modulate at the bridge ('Polka Dots and Moonbeams' goes from F to A; 'Body and Soul' in C goes from D♭ to E in the bridge).

Cycle of 5th harmony is very common in popular song chord progressions and this, and other aspects of chords, are dealt with in the Appendices.

Melody

The melodies of popular songs are most often based on 2-bar phrases, most commonly in the form of 2-bar motifs; 2-bar answering phrase; 2-bar motif repeated; new answering phrase. 'I Got Rhythm' follows this form exactly – even in the bridge.

There is often melodic as well as harmonic contrast between the sections of a popular song: there can be contrast in activity, more or less rhythmic movement, contrast in direction, one starting high and descending, the other low and ascending, contrast in accent, consistent downbeat phrases contrasting with consistent upbeat phrases.

Jazz improvisers rarely play the melodies of popular songs exactly as written. They will *paraphrase* them – adding their own inflexions and treating the melody in a very individual way. This can be seen very clearly on the Lecture Concert Records. Many improvisers feel that a knowledge of the lyrics is essential before they can play the melody successfully: that the words establish the mood, and they improvise as much on the mood as on the melody and/or chord progression. Others, particularly those of the bop era like Charlie Parker, regard the melody purely as the provider of the chord sequence and once the initial statement is over the melody is forgotten. Even in the initial statement there is often a lot of improvising – as though the soloist can't wait to get away from the basic tune. Players like Thelonious Monk feel that the melody is important ('why should we throw it away and only improvise on the background') and make strong use of it in their solos, recognisably repeating and developing fragments of the basic tune.

The lyrics of popular songs have often been fairly banal – excepting the work of Johnny Mercer, Noel Coward, Cole Porter and a very few others. This has been put forward as a possible reason why there are so few singers of *jazz*. Many – like Frank Sinatra – use jazz inflexions in their voices, phrasing the *melodies* in a jazz way. Very few go beyond that and *re-compose*, make something new from the original, as Joe Goldberg said in his *Jazz Masters of the Fifties*, 'trying to make someone else's story their own'. Perhaps the greatest exponent of that in jazz was Billie Holiday.

REFERENCES

LISTENING

A comparison of different musicians playing the same popular song.
Good versions of popular song on the *Anthology* include
  'I Got Rhythm' – Don Redman.
  'Oh! Lady Be Good' – Lester Young. (Starts with improvising.)
  'Round About Midnight' – Thelonius Monk. (A jazz standard.)
  'I've Got You Under My Skin' – J. J. Johnson.
  'All of Me' – Duke Ellington, featuring Johnny Hodges.
  'Mean to Me' – Billie Holiday.

FURTHER READING

American Popular Song, The Great Innovators by Alec Wilder (Oxford University Press). Wilder, himself a good songwriter, explores thoroughly, and warmly, songs and songwriters from 1900 to 1950.

PRACTICAL

Improvising on popular songs

Improvising on chords is a matter of constructing a melody over the chords and observing the nature of each.

Before this can be done effectively chords should be learnt individually – every chord type on every note until all the chord notes are *known* immediately a symbol is seen.

Some possible exercises to achieve this would be:

(basic chord notes going around any of the cycles – 5ths, tones, semitones etc.)

(different chord types on each note)

(different chords starting on the same note).

Patterns

As can be seen in Appendix II certain patterns often recur in many popular songs and the movements in these patterns should be learnt in the same way as the blues patterns were learnt earlier. Possible bass lines can be derived for each pattern.

The various techniques developed for motif and chord improvising can be used.

Illustrations Record track 7 shows chordal improvising over the pattern above. If extra practice is needed the patterns can be played with two bars to each chord.

Once the patterns are familiar at 1 bar to a chord they should be tried at ½ a bar to each chord. (This is the usual way they are seen in popular songs.)

The patterns of Appendix II should then be joined together and similar exercises developed.

Many popular song chord progressions can be made up by joining these patterns together. 'I Got Rhythm' for example is a combination of two patterns in the first 8 bars and a cycle of 5ths round dominant chords in the bridge. Again bass lines can be derived to outline these changes.

Once again familiarity should be gained with the chords and then improvisation tried on that sequence and on the sequences of other popular song progressions.

Again also, backings should be played and riffs developed by the other members of the band.

Illustrations Record track 8 has the band playing on the 'I Got Rhythm' sequence, including some made up backings and riffs.

Tape track 6 has the rhythm section playing the chord progression of 'I Got Rhythm'.

Tape track 7 has the rhythm section playing the chord progression of 'What's New?' which contains some temporary modulations:

F	Bb7	Eb−7	Ab7	Db	Gb7	G−7b5	C7b9	|
F−	Ab7	G−7b5	C7b9	F	Ab7	Db7	Gb7	||
F	Bb7	Eb−7	Ab7	Db	Gb7	G−7b5	C7b9	|
F−	Ab7	G−7b5	C7b9	F	Db7	Gb7	B7	||
Bb	Eb7	Ab−7	Db9	Gb	B7	C−7b5	F7b9	|
Bb−	Db7	C−7b5	F7b9	Bb−	Ab7	Db7	C7	||
F	Bb7	Eb−7	Ab7	Db	Gb7	G−7b5	C7b9	|
F−	Ab7	G−7b5	C7b9	F	Ab7	Db7	Gb7	||

As has been mentioned many popular song chord progressions are based on a combination of such patterns – although the connection may be obscured by unclear writing (for a list of common faults see Appendix II) or by the use of substitute chords (see Appendix III for a list of common substitutes).

Progressions that do not fit into an accepted pattern will have to be learnt in isolation, although once several such oddities are known, connections will be seen.

Using the melody

The melody of a 'standard' song can be used in several ways.

1. It can simply be paraphrased – interpreted in an individual way. This is generally reserved for the initial theme statement when played by a solo instrument.

2. It can be referred to occasionally within the solo (landmarks).

3. It can provide the basis for a complete solo, the soloist exploring different fragments of the tune.

A useful exercise would be to have one soloist play the tune (reasonably as written) and have another improvise around the melody – trying not to get in the way. This can be heard at the end of track 13 on the Illustrations Record.

Also, as with the earlier exercises the melody could be played for the first 2 or 4 bars of an 8-bar section and the remainder of the 8 be improvised.

All of these approaches should be used on various popular songs.

12 Arranging

Perhaps a better term for arranging – which implies some sort of written framework known as 'the arrangement' – would be 'organising' as there is no necessity in many cases for the framework to be written down. The organising can be worked out on the spot and memorised by the musicians involved. If the musicians themselves are adept enough they can do their own organising immediately before or during a performance. The most basic level of this is in the 'blowing groups' of jazz where the theme is played in unison at the beginning and end, and the length and order of the solos between are determined spontaneously. (In all cases though try to avoid every piece featuring every soloist in the same order and all at the same dynamic level. Always try for variety.)

A more advanced form is shown in the aptly named 'head-arrangement's most common in swing era big bands where one man would start to play a repetitive phrase (a riff) and others in the section (i.e. trumpets or trombones or saxes) would join in until there would perhaps be three separate levels of riffs going on. The chord progressions used were very simple and the riffs were such that they would easily fit over each change of chord – possibly by transposition (up a 4th in bar 5 and 6 of the blues for example) or by altering one note. More advanced versions of this spontaneous arranging are seen in contemporary jazz and are dealt with in Chapter 16.

Written arranging as such can cover a range from the notation of a theme, to ensure that all involved know the melody and are using the same set of chords, through the organisation of solo-order and length, with written background to the solos, to a complex multi-layered re-composition.

REFERENCES

LISTENING

Comparisons between arrangements of well known tunes will show some of the possibilities.

When comparing arrangements with other versions or the original listen for:

1. changes in feeling or style
2. changes in form
3. changes from original pitch, if known; try to deduce the reason
4. interesting ideas:
    changes in melodic line
    use of backgrounds; are they derived from the main tune or separately composed?
    interesting textures; try to work out the component factors
    use of introductions and endings
    use of the rhythm section.

(Such analytical listening will assist appreciation as well as one's own arranging.)

The *Anthology* includes interesting versions of

'I Got Rhythm' – Don Redman.
'Stompin' at The Savoy' – Chick Webb.
'Tickle Toe' – Count Basie.
'Four Brothers' – Woody Herman.
'Yardbird Suite' – Claude Thornhill.
'All of Me' – Duke Ellington.

Compare the three small group arrangements (tracks 52, 53, 54) for the interest in texture, form, etc.

FURTHER READING

Sounds and Scores by Henry Mancini.

PRACTICAL

Choice of key

Before writing out even the simplest theme for a group of musicians steps must be taken to ensure that it is in a favourable key for the instrumentalists involved. This is dependent on their individual technical facility but a general guide to suitable ranges would be within a 3rd of either end of the accepted range of the instrument. (Appendix VI carries a list of these plus a guide to transpositions.)

The choice of key is controlled by

1. technical facility (again taking transposition into account)
2. common practice
3. the 'sound' of each possible key.

The most common keys used in jazz are, not surprisingly when one

remembers possible transpositions, B♭, F and C. Standard songs however should, wherever possible, be left in their original key (that of the
sheet music). If this is not possible or the key is not known the only
satisfactory way is by trial and error. A few bars of the melody played
on the piano in each viable key should give enough flavour for a
decision to be made – but one must always of course pay heed to any
necessary instrumental transpositions.

Chord progressions

Many lead sheets (melodies and chords written out) and song copies
have chord progressions which would be easier to read, understand
and play from if they were (a) simplified and (b) correctly written with
regard to their function in the key. A list of common faults will be
found in Appendix II.

Such chord progressions can often be improved by the use of
substitute chords to relieve the monotony of a repeated chord,
heighten or lessen tension, provide a stronger bass line etc. A list of
substitute chords will be found in Appendix III.

Simple arrangements

These can best be achieved by giving each member of the band a lead
sheet – transposed if necessary.

Collier – 'The Barley Mow'

These can form the basis for a verbal arrangement on the lines of 'all in
on the theme, 1 chorus alto solo, 1 chorus trumpet solo, all in on the
theme to end'.

If it's done this way there can be a fresh approach each time; each
try can be different. The musicians also get early practice in memoris-
ing the form. Melody and chords are written together in order that the
musician can always see and hear the connection between the two and
use them both in his own solo. Not too skilled improvisers can also *use*
the theme as the basis for their solo.

Where possible these lead sheets should be memorised, perhaps
during one week, for performance at the next session.

NB Jazz quavers are written as straight quavers (♪). One expects the musicians to interpret them in a jazz way. Writing them in 12/8 or as triplets ♩ ♪ or as ♩. ♩ only complicates matters. *If* absolutely straight quavers are required in a jazz situation it is usually enough to write 'even♪s' over the passage in question and 'jazz♪s' *at the next written part.*

Adaptations of simple arrangements

By change at each performance as mentioned.

By incorporating parts of the theme at each chorus, possibly bars 1–4 at the start of each chorus. An adaptation of this would be to use bars 1/2 on one chorus, 3/4 on the next and so on. This would at least keep all the band awake!

By having the musicians create patterns on chords. These could range from organ-like sustained chords to riffs, as discussed in Chapters 10 and 11. These could be prearranged or left to be worked out in performance, possibly by one player leading and the others following.

Using the rhythm section in simple arrangements

Generally the rhythm players should be given lead sheets the same as the others, even the drummer – a knowledge of the melody is of importance to him also. Some indication should probably be given of the style required (brushes or sticks, 2-beat or 4-beat), dynamics and any changes of mood, but in that the rhythm section's role is largely improvisatory it is best to give them a guide rather than specify.

Appendix V deals with the use of piano, guitar bass and drums as a rhythm section.

More complex arrangements

These can be derived by building from a simple arrangement – perhaps by adding to it week after week. They can of course also be written, and this will probably involve the use of voicings, backgrounds and contrapuntal melodies.

Voicings are covered more specifically in Chapter 13 on big bands, and smaller group voicings are best adapted from them. However some specific hints for small group writing are:

1. Use the piano to complete front line voicings.

2. Use the piano left hand and bass on counterlines.

3. Vary front line textures. Use unisons when the melody is active; use voicings on accented notes and long notes; write separate melodic lines, either as counterpoint or as answering phrases.

The writing of backgrounds

1. The background should be sufficiently different to be apart from the melody, but should also complement it.

2. When the melody moves sustain or rest the background. When the melody is sustained or silent the background usually moves more.

3. Avoid using important melody notes in the background near their use in the melody.

4. Keep background within an octave of the melody and not less than a 3rd away when background and melody attack together.

5. Avoid rhythmic confusion by having melody and background anticipate together, i.e. *not*

6. Do not use backgrounds all the time.

7. When used behind an improvised solo backgrounds should where possible be written on the part of the soloist.

Common background ideas

1. sustained or activated lines from the chords
2. answering phrases
3. ostinato figures
4. jazz solo background
5. percussive accents.

Contrapuntal lines

Counterpoint is sparked off by a close study of the piece and a certain amount of inspiration. After this the process seems to be a matter of trial and error. As will be mentioned later, though, ideas can be inspired by already written material. The melody of one section may provide a counterpoint to the melody of another. The following example shows a counterpoint derived from the augmentation of the original theme.

Such counterpoints can be used as a backing to a solo passage first, then later as a proper counterpoint to the melody.

Imagination

Imagination is probably the greatest attribute an arranger can have:

The imagination to see that the rhythm section are treated as part of the band – not simply as machines banging out an insistent pulse with no change of texture or dynamics. It should be remembered that

1. there are a variety of ways of playing the pulse – 4 beats to a bar; 2 beats to a bar; latin american feel; double time etc.;

2. the use of bass alone, drums alone or even piano alone can be very effective, as can the build-up of a passage perhaps with bass plus soloist on theme first, then with piano added and then with drums;

3. you can create a good effect by stopping something after it is established; stop time choruses are the classic example of this;

4. the drums can be used colourfully, for example the use of just one cymbal, tambourine or maracas to play the actual pulse. (See Appendix V for further suggestions.)

The imagination to see new possibilities in a tune such as a new tempo, a new way of treating a tune or a new tune signature for all or part of it. In all cases, especially the last, the resultant arrangement must sound natural, not forced into a mould but as though *that* were the original way. Don Sebesky's treatment of 'I Feel Pretty' from *West Side Story* as a gospel number is brilliant; Bill Potts' decision to treat 'Summertime' as an up-tempo number was far less successful.

The imagination to see that much (if not all) of the additional material for your arrangement can be derived from the original theme, thus giving it a continuity which may not always be immediately apparent but which affects the totality of the performance. (The techniques of this are covered in Chapter 15.)

The imagination to re-compose the basic material, perhaps by paraphrasing the melody or – at some point in the arrangement – writing a new melody over the established chords or providing a new chord sequence for the original melody.

The imagination to vary the *weight* of the instrumentation – to give rests to the musicians and the listener.

The imagination to vary colour by using mutes, doubling instruments and using instruments in new ranges or unusual mixtures. In the latter case it is as well to have an idea to fall back on in case the new one fails to work in the time available. This can be a mental note that it *would* work by taking the mute off or dropping it an octave, or it may be the precaution of having the passage copied out on another musician's music.

The imagination to select the people best suited for particular functions – don't use them 'because they haven't played for a while'.

The imagination to move away from the traditional theme–solos–theme form: possibly by incorporating new interlude material; dispensing with the initial theme statement; finishing only with part of the theme, or having the soloist use only *part* of the chord progression.

The imagination to try to *involve* all the musicians: by making up riffs as in head arrangements; by allowing the soloist to determine the length of his own solos; by allowing the rhythm section to determine their own dynamics and textures, etc.

The imagination to start – and particularly *end* – your arrangement in an imaginative way.

The mechanics

Work on scores in pencil (for ease of erasure).

Copy the actual parts as legibly as possible in ink (waterproof to avoid it washing away as spit falls from water keys!).

Give each player as much as possible of what's going on in the way of cues. This makes it easier for beginners to know where they are and enables changes to be made easily between parts.

Write chords for solos as simple as possible, *but* containing all the alterations enforced by the backing, e.g. if the chord is F7 and the backing includes B♮ the soloist's part needs to be written as 'F7 (♯11)'.

Indicate the duration of chords (or alterations) by virgules for each beat.

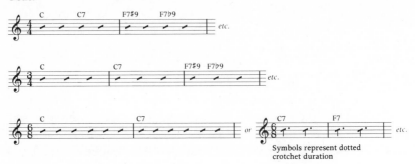

Write in dynamics (and make sure they are played).

The drummer should be given a sketch part telling him what is going on. If specific rhythms need to be written they should be written according to the following

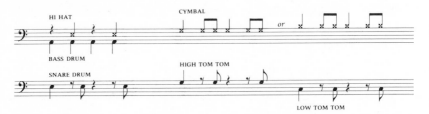

Tom-toms should be marked if used. The hi-hat is not normally written in. Always stipulate brushes or sticks. (Appendix V gives some basic hints.)

Piano and bass should either be given specific parts or chord symbols with virgules. Care should be taken not to restrict them by overwriting.

Markings

Controversy exists over correct markings. Fairly common are ∧ for a short, not too short, detached note, and — over the note for a long, full value, note; > is used for accented notes.

Consistency is all-important.

Illustrations Record track 9 has an example of imaginative arranging. It is part of a long composition called 'Portraits I' and it uses the members of the group and the featured soloist on flugelhorn in a variety of ways: as players of the main melody; to improvise freely; to improvise behind the melody; to improvise with another player, and so on. Note also the use of guitar and piano in the group. A full version of this composition is available on *Portraits* (Saydisc) and the scores are also available.

13 The big band

The big band in jazz traditionally consists of around 16 players – 4 trumpets, 3 or 4 trombones, 5 saxophones (2 altos, 2 tenors and a baritone) and a 3 or 4 piece rhythm section (piano, bass, drums, and sometimes guitar). Traditionally also, the writing for such big bands utilises, in a 'pure' way, those instrumental sections. In other words melodies and countermelodies are played by the trumpets en masse, trombones en masse or saxophones en masse or by a combination of two sections (saxes and trombones; trumpets and trombones) or all three (ensemble): voicings made *across* the sections, two trumpets, sax and trombone for example, are relatively rare. The content of the arrangements is straightforward with many of the lines based on the call and response patterns derived from work songs and negro religious services where a statement from one section is answered by a statement from another section. The form of such arrangements is usually based on the repetition of the basic structure, with possible modulations. There is usually no thematic development as such.

In other words the complete structure, instrumentation, orchestration, content and form, for the majority of big bands in jazz is predictable.

This is not to say that such a style is not valid and indeed it has its use in certain situations today.

The heyday of such bands, however, was in the swing era of the late thirties and the style originated with the arrangements of Don Redman for Fletcher Henderson's band. The style was thoroughly explored by the bands of Jimmie Lunceford, Henderson himself and Benny Goodman, who became a great commercial success and was called the 'King of Swing'.

Contemporary big bands who work within that style – often with the trappings of a rock beat and electric instruments – include Buddy Rich and Woody Herman and while such bands can be exciting, there is little of musical interest left once the excitement has worn off. There is educational value in playing some arrangements of this genre – the need for the band to phrase as one and the sheer excitement of the faster pieces – but over-concentration on this style of playing can lead to sterility. The form is no longer valid except as a tiny part of the whole and to concentrate on it exclusively as some 'jazz educationalists' do is to ignore the fact that jazz should be a *creative* music and that the heyday of this style is as far away from us *now* as the beginnings of jazz were from it.

Duke Ellington, though, explored this traditional big band style in a more creative way. He has, generally, used a traditional big band instrumentation (4 trumpets, 3 trombones, 5 saxes, piano, bass and drums) but the range of textures he draws from it is remarkable. This is because he treats each instrumentalist as an individual – not simply as one trumpet player out of four, but as a separate human being – and he exploits the individual tones and resources of his players to build a constantly altering texture, voicing almost always *across* the sections rather than *within* them as the other bands did. The content of his arrangements is freer also. If the call and response patterns are used it will often be with a band phrase answered by an improvised fill from a soloist – and such improvisations keep the arrangement sounding fresh. The textures will often change from phrase to phrase rather than at the end of 8- or 12-bar sections which conform with the basic structure.

The forms used, though they are most often *based* on the repetition of the basic structure will include interludes and new melodies to give the arrangement freshness and continuity. Within the conventional 3–5 minute length (derived from the length of a single record) a remarkable degree of compositional development is shown.

Ellington's style then is *creative* within the conventions of the big band and because of this it is less easy to recreate than, say, that of the Count Basie band. Its sound depends on the utilisation of the individual characteristics of its instrumentalists; without them the sound will be different. An attempt could be made to capture those sounds by imitation but it is more valuable to apply Ellington's ideas to fresh writing or the rearrangement of standard material.

Ellington apart, opportunities for creative big band writing since the war have been limited by the economics of the jazz business. Few bands have existed outside the recording studio; this raises considerable problems regarding the working-in of arrangements, and the writer can very rarely get to know the individuals on the band sufficiently well. (Writers do use the same musicians on each recording as far as possible.) The most interesting work in contemporary big bands has been done by Gil Evans, Gerry Mulligan, Charles Mingus and Mike Gibbs. Of these Evans particularly has enlarged the instrumental possibilities of jazz by incorporating into his writing such instruments as the flute, oboe, bassoon, french horn and harp.

REFERENCES

LISTENING

Duke Ellington – see Chapter 2. Also 'Black and Tan Fantasy' (1927), 'Primpin' for the Prom' (1952) and 'All of Me' (1959) are on the *Anthology*.
Fletcher Henderson – 'Sugarfoot Stomp' (1925), *Anthology*.
Jimmie Lunceford – 'T'aint What You Do' (1939), *Anthology*.
Benny Goodman – 'King Porter Stomp' (1937), arranged by Henderson, and 'Solo Flight', *Anthology*.
Count Basie – 'Tickle Toe' (1940) and 'Little Pony' (1951), *Anthology*.
Woody Herman – 'Four Brothers' (1947), with three tenor saxes and a baritone.
Claude Thornhill – 'Yardbird Suite' (1947), composed by Parker, arranged by Gil Evans, *Anthology*.
Gil Evans – 'Springsville' (1957), arranged by Evans, *Anthology*.

PRACTICAL

Some hints on rehearsing

Always run through the piece first, preferably at its correct tempo. This enables the piece to be seen as a whole and often avoids wasteful rehearsal. For example if the band all have a theme but at different parts of the arrangement, it may save time to have them all play it together (make sure it hasn't modulated though!). Also, a later passage may be a complex version of an earlier theme and rehearsal of it may save going through the simpler passage at all. Rehearsal of one after the other may help too – and may also assist the musicians to see the connection.

Stop everyone tapping their feet (especially if audible) and get them to count *mentally* in 2. It is easier to count in 2 than 4 and less likely to lead to confusion – particularly on passages such as

Rehearse the sections without the lead player. Many section musicians hide behind a strong lead and though they might be afraid to play on their own completely, this method will help isolate a major problem – the lack of *body* in a section. Student bands generally sound thin because of this lack of body in the different sections and the problem can be easily seen by isolating the inner members of the section in this way.

Try percussive chords first as a sustained sound then as written and try to get the same density of sound. Such chords are often voiced in a dissonant way and the dissonances will not come out if all the parts are not played *solidly* – every man, and particularly those on the bottom of the band, playing his note fully and accurately. These percussive chords are often seen as a pick up (as in the last example),

and are marked to be played with an attack and short, but the chord is seldom given its full weight. If it is played wrongly it should be rehearsed in three stages

(a) sustained

(b) as a percussive note (but *full*)

(c) as written

and care should be taken to ensure that the body of the dissonance is the same each time. These techniques, while welcomed by musicians during rehearsal, are often forgotten in the heat of a straight run through. Whenever possible the point should be rehearsed again immediately.

When rehearsing make sure that not too much time is spent on one section as it tires its members out and may irritate the others – who should however be told to listen and learn from *all* the rehearsal, not just the parts that specifically affect them.

Passages like

need careful rehearsing in that the inner voices of the harmony parts need to be played louder to give equal weight to the whole passage.

The rhythm section should normally play all the time while separate sections are being rehearsed (but should play simply and quietly). Occasionally though it may be worthwhile to try the whole band without the rhythm section as they should be able to swing on their own.

Solo passages should be tried over for the sake of the soloist and the rhythm section (but this could be done immediately before or after an interval without inconveniencing the others).

Fast tempo numbers should be tried through up to tempo *immediately*, if there is a chance that some of the band will make it. This gives an idea of the dimensions of the problem to the others who are often amazed at how easy it all seems after a steadier tempoed rehearsal to attain the previously impossible tempo. Each difficult passage should be slowed down and rehearsed but each subsequent run-through should be slightly faster until the original tempo is reached. If time is limited, however, bear in mind that it is better to play 8 bars *right* as the composer wanted than to make a bad stab at the whole number.

With slow tempos, one of the commonest faults in big bands is failing to feel a slow tempo correctly. Almost all big bands have Count Basie's 'Li'l Darling' in their library but very few – if any – can play it without speeding up and without several different ideas as to exactly where the beat is. Passages like

should be rehearsed softly to try to make everyone feel them together, and to retain the *intensity* at a low dynamic level.

Attention to dynamic markings should always be stressed, as should the desirability of all the band being able to hear the lead or soloist.

It is often useful to rehearse an ensemble passage without the drums or without the lead trumpet, and it is generally advisable to rehearse the backing to a solo without the soloist actually playing. It lets him hear what's happening behind him, and lets you hear it clearly.

Keep ringing the changes to keep the band awake and aware of how the piece is constructed.

Repertoire

One of the major problems with the big band is repertoire. Much of the material lacks *involvement*. Where possible already written material should be adapted to take this into account and to make it more personal. Some possibilities would be to

1. Lengthen the solos by the insertion of extra choruses, either a pre-arranged number, a number dictated by the soloist himself in performance, or a number determined by the bandleader bringing in a backing on the soloist's final chorus.

2. Solos can be changed around within the band – either by straight swapping of parts between trumpets for example or a quick copying of the relevant chords for another instrument entirely. Always be careful though that the same people do not take the solos all the time. Ideally everyone in the band should get an equal chance.

3. Some arrangements may be improved by complete restructuring. Omitting repeats, inserting new repeats, leaving passages out, playing them again at the end etc.

Voicings

To cover big band voicings in the space available is obviously impossible and a close study of some scores will suggest various possibilities. However it may be useful to clarify ensemble writing methods here.

Concerted (for passages which move but do not have too much range or too many skips).

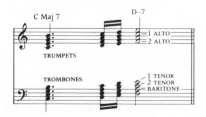

Saxes coupled with brass. Lead alto within

Tutti (for passages which move less, where chords have a chance to establish themselves).

Saxes, wider voicings. Lead alto within

Four note ensemble (best for solo like melodies which are not too complex).

Trombones an octave below. Saxes coupled with brass.

Unison (best if the line is very complex and/or very strong).

Percussive ensemble (best for accented chords. Possible if there are many repeated notes.)

(Tensions are used *inside* the chord. Saxes are coupled.) The various methods can be mixed within a passage as long as the music calls for it.

Low intervals: to avoid muddy voicings try not to go outside these limits for the lowest interval

This applies to the two lowest notes of the voicing and also the interval between the lowest note of the voicing and the root of the chord – whether it is there or not.

For example

obeys the rules while

breaks the rules because of the 'implied root' (implied by the rhythm section or the voicings used).

14 Modes and scales

As soon as an improviser starts to use passing notes when constructing his solo – either diatonic

or using some of the possible additions and alterations

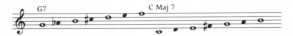

– he is improvising using scales, and the approach has been common in jazz since the time of Lester Young. A progression like

B♭ G−7 C−7 F7

suggests the same scales for each chord, although starting on a different root,

and an improviser will treat that pattern as a tonal area.

Working from this approach in his re-composition of Gershwin's score to *Porgy and Bess*, Gil Evans broke away from the original harmonic scheme and asked Miles Davis to improvise on a scale (in 'I Loves You Porgy') and on one or two chords only (in parts of 'I Loves You Porgy' and 'Summertime'). This later led Davis himself to produce *Kind of Blue*, a series of compositions written specifically for a recording session to make use of various aspects of the scalic approach to improvising.

Davis was reacting, as Ornette Coleman was at the same time though working completely independently, against the increasing complexity, both horizontal and vertical, of chord progression in the bop and post bop periods. Chords were so complex and tempos often so fast that there was often little one could do to create musical solos from them.

There was also the problem of repetition of the structure. As Miles Davis said, at the end of 32 bars 'there's nothing to do but repeat what you've just done with variations'. This of course could be considered to be part of the challenge of improvisation – to see how you can *develop* an idea from chorus to chorus – and scalic improvising did not suddenly make chordal progressions invalid as the basis for solos.

What did happen though was that chord progressions were simplified and that a break was made with the diatonically based cycle of 5ths progressions that had predominated up to that time.

Improvisers were freed from the horizontal aspect of the music, the chord structures, and left to concentrate on the vertical aspect, the melody. As Davis said, 'It becomes a challenge to see how melodically inventive you can be', and he prophesied, 'I think a movement in jazz is beginning away from the conventional string of chords and a return to emphasis on melodic rather than harmonic variation. There will be fewer chords but infinite possibilities as to what to do with them.'

Modes

One of the most influential pieces on *Kind of Blue* was 'So What', a simple bass statement/band answer melody in a conventional AABA 32-bar form. The difference was that the piece was constructed in the Dorian mode (white notes of the piano starting on D) with the 'B' section transposed up a ½ step (E♭, F, G♭, A♭, B♭, C, D♭, E♭). This gave a great sense of space to the improvisation as instead of chord changes every bar or half bar as in a normal piece, the 32-bar structure only had two changes.

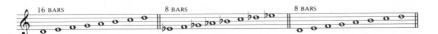

Miles himself sticks very close to the scale, while tenor saxophonist John Coltrane roams much further afield, using passing notes and accidentals to create tension with the basic harmony, thus starkly showing two of the 'infinite possibilities' Davis mentioned.

This use of modes prompted many similar compositions, usually in the Dorian mode, but sometimes the Phrygian or Aeolian, either obviously on one scale, on two chords that implied a scale (II−7

V7 (D—7 G7 in C) implying the Dorian mode, as 'So What', or on a modal progression. These progressions used the modal structure freely and could be improvised on by using the mode only

Collier – 'The Barley Mow'. (Note the change of mode in the bridge.)

Other scales

'Flamenco Sketches' from *Kind of Blue* used specially written scales in a much freer way. There is no melody as such and the soloists were presented with five scales and told to improvise on each scale as long as they liked and then move to the next. This presents a considerable challenge to the improviser to be inventive within the limits of the scale, as venturing too far away from the notes of one scale will cause confusion with the others.

The approach inherent in 'So What' freed improvisers from the restrictions of a chord progression; the approach inherent in 'Flamenco Sketches' freed improvisers and composers from the restrictions of a recurring form, and Ornette Coleman's experiments were leading jazz in a parallel direction. If there were no melody or chord progression to set up a form (as in 'Flamenco Sketches') then the improvising could last as long as the soloist wanted; if the melody had no supporting chord structure (as in Ornette Coleman's work) then the improviser could develop that melody freely, either within the general tonal area or moving outside it.

These parallel developments also considerably affected the whole future of composition. Freedom from the restrictions of a repetitive chord progression and a recurring form gave composers new opportunities which revitalised the music.

REFERENCES

LISTENING

Porgy and Bess (CBS) – Miles Davis and Gil Evans.
Kind of Blue (CBS) – Miles Davis.
'The Barley Mow' on *Down Another Road* (Fontana) and *Jazz in the Classroom,*
   Volume VII (Berklee Records) – Graham Collier Sextet.

PRACTICAL

Improvising with scales and modes

Apart from some new possibilities for scale notes there is little difference in improvising on chords using passing notes as we have done before, or improvising using scales.

For example, a purely diatonic progression could be thought of as one scale. Either the major scale or the Dorian mode.

But if it were to continue

then there will have been a temporary modulation and the scale used for those bars would be

However if it were to return to C

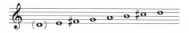

then there would be two choices to use over the E−7 chord as it could be in either key.

The choice would be clear if there were a melody at that point but if there is no melody it's a matter of personal inclination – possibly a combination of each would be used to suggest the modulation

Passing non-diatonic chords such as secondary dominants generally use the diatonic mode altered where the chord note is altered

Ensemble exercises similar to those used already should be adapted to incorporate this.

Other scales can be used and these are often more difficult to handle. A list of these with some suggested uses is given in Appendix VII and these should be learnt individually before being used in an improvising situation. A possible exercise would be to have the rhythm section repeat a chord for 8 bars while one scale is used, then try another scale on the same chord, etc. The choice of scale depends on the individual.

Illustrations Record track 10 has the rhythm section playing a G7 chord while a soloist plays on a straightforward scale (G,A,B,C,D,E,F), an altered scale (G,A♭,B♭,B♮,D♭,E♭,F) and a whole tone scale.

This is good practice for improvising for long periods on a single scale. The main problem is getting sufficient melodic and rhythmic interest from the one scale. Often such scales do have an implied harmony – D–7 for D Dorian for example – but it is best to try to forget chordal connections where possible.

Illustrations Record track 11 has a soloist and rhythm section playing on a Dorian mode.

Tape track 8 has the rhythm section playing on a Dorian mode and on *track 9* on a Phrygian mode.

Some hints are given for the rhythm section in Appendix V.

Harmonisation within scales and modes

This is best done in diatonic voicings from the scale, i.e. if the melody is from

then the chords are

(Normally the V7 of the key is avoided.) Or one can find a suitable sound from the scale and voice in strict parallelism. For example

is in C minor and could be voiced

A piece that has been specifically written within a mode loses its charm when harmonised outside the mode. The original harmonisation:

A possible non-modal harmonisation:

Incomplete scales like the pentatonic can be used to express several different modalities.

An extension of this approach was used in the bridge of 'The Barley Mow' (see p. 124) where the melody stays in D Dorian and the harmonisation is from G Dorian, the same scale but with a B♭ — which is not used in the melody.

15   Jazz composition

The material used in jazz to provide the framework for improvisation, can be divided into two main sections, one much larger than the other. •The larger section is that of theme (and possible arrangement of that theme) where the soloist is supreme; the smaller is composition – where the theme has been developed in some way and where the soloist is subordinate. The distinction between the two is blurred at times, and as we shall see there can be excellent development even on a small theme, but it provides a basis for examining the whole field of jazz composition in its two basic aspects – what is improvised and what is written. It is the successful joining of these two elements that concerns almost all jazz musicians.

This joining is very often simply a matter of harmonic connection between the two parts: the improvising uses the same chord progression as the theme. The melody itself is forgotten during the solo passages, and is used merely to state that chord progression, set up a tempo and establish a mood.

Taken by themselves such themes can be good melodies, 'Round about Midnight', for example, or simply repetitive motifs like 'So What' or 'One O'Clock Jump', but the performance stands or falls on the excellence of the soloist's imagination.

With some composers, though, the joining between what is written and what is improvised becomes more interesting. Thelonius Monk's tunes for example are generally developed from one specific motif – his 'Straight No Chaser' is a brilliant example of rhythmic displacement of the initial motif. His improvising is *also* concerned with the melody and there is no doubt with Monk – even when he is using 12-bar blues harmonies – which theme he is improvising on.

The first jazz composer was Jelly Roll Morton, whose writing was strongly influenced by ragtime, where there were several themes. His soloists were quite strictly controlled – indeed some of the earlier solos were written out – but the overall result was unquestionably jazz, it had freshness and spontaneity, and equally unquestionably composition, with development between and within the sections.

Morton's work – perhaps because of its strong ragtime influence – was not tremendously influential and other writers, while generally paying lip-service to him, have rarely followed on from his ideas. The man whose influence is paramount in jazz writing is of course Duke Ellington and it seems that all worthwhile developments in jazz composition can be traced back to him.

In Ellington's work and in that of his *alter-ego* Billy Strayhorn the soloist is not permitted to run wild. He has been chosen for what he can add to the composition and his contribution is carefully controlled. A fairly obvious example of this is Strayhorn's 'Chelsea Bridge' where the solo spots are given to Lawrence Brown and Ben Webster – two players whose romantic lyricism and 'breathy' tones add to the impressionistic approach that Strayhorn was trying for.

The form is carefully controlled also. There is a sense of development and of continuity throughout – even in a 3-minute composition.

Perhaps one of the finest short compositions in jazz is John Lewis's 'Django' (written as an elegy for Django Reinhardt). It is all constructed from the initial 2-bar motif which is later developed into two separate parts, each of which is then explored. It manages to capture the strange mixture of sadness and rejoicing shown in the New Orleans funeral traditions. The improvising takes place on a separate, though loosely derived, chord progression.

Since the late 1950s there has been an increasing trend towards longer *compositions* as opposed to series of smaller pieces linked together into suites. Often the creative impetus has been derived from straight music and the resultant music, 'third stream', lacks the freshness of jazz. As critic Gene Lees has said, 'Third stream tends to impose form on jazz from without, rather than building it from within.' One of the most successful long works in jazz, Charles Mingus's 'Meditations on Integration', has passages which could almost be straight music, a three-way improvisation between flute, bowed bass and piano, for example, but it stems directly from the piece as a whole. It has not been imposed from outside.

The most difficult problem in jazz composition is of course to integrate soloists into the fabric of the composer's design. Obviously they will have been carefully chosen but even then there is the possibility that their solo will not fulfil the composer's requirements. This of course does not arise if the piece is sufficiently free for the performers to contribute to the composition, but if the piece is trying to express the composer's thoughts – either abstract or programmatic – then the soloist must be even more prepared to subordinate himself to the piece than he would otherwise be. This implies restriction of the soloist's personality but as Miles Davis shows in 'Saeta' (from *Sketches of Spain*) this can be turned to supreme advantage. Gil Evans put Miles into a situation where he represented a Spanish woman singer in the midst of a religious procession. The finished performance is a superb example of how a great soloist, while subordinating himself to the *demands* of a composer, can still play brilliantly. His portrayal of the singer is eminently believable and is still jazz. It shows the way to a new level of jazz composition where composer and soloist combine to portray an idea outside jazz, away from the basic *separateness* of theme and solos composition or the integration of improvisation and solos to portray an idea *within* accepted jazz traditions.

REFERENCES

LISTENING

'Django' on *The Modern Jazz Quartet* (Prestige).
'Round about Midnight' – Thelonius Monk, *Anthology*.
'Meditations on Integration' on *Mingus at Monterey* (America).
'Saeta' on *Sketches of Spain* (CBS).
Part 1 of 'Darius' on the Lecture Concert Record, a contemporary composition, integrates improvisation and pre-composition.
Other good jazz compositions are
George Russell – 'All about Rosie' (featuring an incredible piano solo by Bill Evans), *Anthology*.
Charles Mingus – *Let My Children Hear Music* (CBS). Includes some good material, and the *Anthology* has 'Gunslinging Bird'.
Carla Bley – *Escalator Over the Hill* (JCOA Records). A fascinating 3-volume mixture of musics.
And of course Duke Ellington.

FURTHER READING

Compositional Devices (based on Songs For My Father) by Graham Collier (Berklee Publications, Boston, 1974).
The Thematic Process in Music by Rudolph Reti (Faber, 1961).

PRACTICAL

Starting from nothing

The basic problem in composing is the actual start – the derivation of
the first motif. This is of course often inspired but there are times when
inspiration is lacking and a piece must be written. At these times one
can fall back on various techniques to derive the initial motif.

1. By numbers – by applying a scale to a group of numbers. E.g.
24.6.73. would give, taking C as '1'.

And a possible motif from these notes would be

NB The sole purpose of the basic motif is to stimulate the mind, and
the example above shows how the basic idea then develops.

2. By letters – applying a scale to a group of letters. E.g. EDWARD
would give

The scale is extended to take account of notes above G. This could give

(Note the alteration of one of the D's)

3. By related ideas. For example an old folk song was used to derive
a complete composition in my 'Smoke Blackened Walls and Curlews'.
The opening was

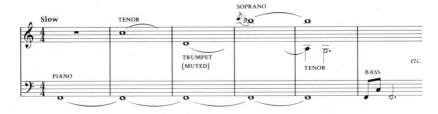

and was derived from

4. From non-musical ideas. Any rhythm or sound outside music can spark off ideas. The following rhythm was heard from a pigeon

and became the basis for the rhythm pattern for 'Gay Talk'.

Once an initial motif has been written – or inspired – it can be developed by repetition or by using an answering phrase. It can also be developed by various other techniques known as transformations – some of which are listed in Appendix VIII.

Another method is to try to write a melody over a given chord progression (either freshly written or that of a standard).

A further discussion of these techniques is given in my *Compositional Devices (based on Songs For My Father)* (Berklee Publications, 1974).

16   Contemporary trends

From its beginnings up until the late 1950s jazz had used the elements
of music in roughly the same way. Harmonies, though they had got
more complex, were basically formed from cycle of 5ths progressions.
Melodies were most often in blues or popular song form and quite
often the music had been composed for other circumstances. The
insistent pulse of jazz rarely faltered and by far the commonest time
signature was 4 beats to a bar, although more complex rhythms were
imposed over this basic pulse as jazz progressed. Development in
arrangements and compositions was most often of the theme–solos–
theme kind.

Since the late fifties players and writers, while still continuing to
work in the older ways, have been finding new ways of looking at all
these aspects.

New melodies

Jazz musicians have concentrated more on writing their own compositions – possibly just a theme and chords but, even so, a *fresh* melody,
possibly angular, relying less on repetition of the basic motif, often
making its point by implication rather than directly, and containing a
higher degree of dissonance.

New harmonies

Many of these melodies are modal and scalic in construction and are
accompanied by a repeated pattern of one or two chords. These
patterns form the *basis* of the rhythm section improvisation; they are
rarely played throughout the piece as written. Many of the chord
based melodies are harmonised freely, by sound rather than following
old patterns based on the cycle of 5ths. Such progressions may
concentrate on one type of chord and move freely between them,
though movements of a tone are common.

New time signatures

There has been a slackening of the insistence on a regular 4/4 pulse in jazz and a trend to give the drummer greater autonomy, to move him from his previous role of time keeper to an equal status with the soloist. The result of this (apart from an increase in volume) was that the pulse was implied rather than stated and was often dropped altogether. And, of course, this was recognised in the new compositions which were written with it in mind.

Composers also started to move away from 4 beats in a bar. Tunes were written which fitted naturally into odd times like Paul Desmond's 'Take Five', but others seemed forced; as one critic said, 'bad jazz is bad jazz whether it's in 4/4 or 11/8'. To make soloing easier on some of these complex times it was stated prominently throughout by an ostinato in the bass or piano or both. Other tunes went into 4/4 for the solo sections.

Some composers have combined various complex times in the basic blues form. My own 'Song Three' from *Songs For My Father* has the following bass pattern, and although at first it proved difficult after a time the soloists were creating quite happily on it.

Illustrations Record track 12 has a short solo on the chords and time structure of 'Song Three'.

New forms

The avant garde has reinstated the collective improvisation tradition common in earlier jazz, but whereas before there was a form and a melody there is often nowadays neither. The collective improvising is done from a pre-set idea or freely created by the musicians following each other. This freedom has also come into more conventional contemporary jazz where two or three soloists may be asked to improvise together over a pattern or chord sequence. Also solo cadenzas can be used to join between sections of a longer composition. These can be all-in or true solos and can be freely improvised, though one would expect the mood to be kept, or controlled as a bridge leading to a new piece.

New sounds

The avant garde has also returned to the more vocalised sounds of earlier jazz. Players such as Roswell Rudd have shown how the earthier aspects of the trombone (glisses, growls, smears etc.) can be utilised in contemporary jazz and saxophone players have extended their range considerably, especially the tenor and, with John Surman, the baritone.

Drummers because of their new creative role have started to use all sorts of instruments to produce interesting sound. Some contemporary percussionists (perhaps a better word) are using electronic drums because of the increased range of sounds offered. Because of the increasing use of amplification in jazz, instruments such as the alto flute and bass clarinet are appearing as solo instruments. Guitars and electric pianos are common and their gadgetry (fuzz boxes, wah wah pedals etc.) are even used with other instruments like the trumpet.

All of these new developments co-exist with older forms and are often intermixed. It is only the extreme avant garde who dismiss the old for the sake of the new. Other players and writers have absorbed these new things into their own individual approach.

REFERENCES

LISTENING

On the *Anthology* the following tracks show contemporary developments:
    'As Catch Can' – Gerry Mulligan (pianoless quartet).

'Sweet Sue' – Miles Davis (modern playing).

'Waltz Limps' – Dave Brubeck (blues in 3/4).

'Gunslinging Bird' – Charles Mingus (participatory arranging by the band).

'Two Bass Hit' – John Coltrane (modern playing on chords).

'Chappaqua Suite' – Ornette Coleman (some modern playing without chords).

My own compositions are listed on p. xiv.

Contemporary sounds on common jazz instruments are demonstrated on the Lecture Concert Record.

PRACTICAL

Improvising on new harmonies

As with the previous material familiarity should be gained by playing through many times before improvisation is attempted. Scales should be applied as suggested earlier.

Illustrations Record track 13 has the band playing on the melody and chord sequence at the beginning of the chapter.

Tape track 10 has the rhythm section playing on that sequence.

Improvising in new time signatures

All time signatures can be broken down into combinations of 2 beats and 3 beats:

3/4 is 3:1 2 3   1 2 3

4/4 is 2+2:1 2 3 4

5/4 is usually 3+2 (though 2+3 is known, it is rare):

  1 2 3 4 5 ('Take Five' is ♪♩ ♪♩ ┊♩ ♩)

6/8 is usually 3+3:1 2 3 4 5 6

6/4 is usually the same but could be 2+2+2:1 2 3 4 5 6

7/4 or 7/8 is usually 2+2+3:1 2 3 4 5 6 7 (Dave Brubeck's 'Unsquare

  Dance' has the offbeats clapped) 1 2̇ 3 4̇ 5 6̇ 7̇

9/8 is usually 3+3+3:1 2 3 4 5 6 7 8 9 (Brubeck's 'Blue Rondo à la Turk' was 2+2+2+3:1 2 3 4 5 6 7 8 9 with an occasional bar as normal).

11/8 is usually 3⅔/4 time 3+3+3+2:1 2 3 4 5 6 7 8 9 10 11

Times over 11/8 can best be written as combinations of times, e.g.

13/8 as $\dfrac{4+4+5}{8}$ and indeed this may be the safer way to write some of the lower values also.

Exercises in time

Ostinatos can be derived for each 'time' and repeated while improvisation is tried over them. Some possibilities would be

and these could be applied to a basic blues sequence

Illustrations Record track 14 shows an improvisation on this pattern.

Tape track 11 has a blues sequence in 3/4; *track 12* a blues in 5/4; *track 13* a blues in 6/8 (6/4); *track 14* a blues in 7/4.

The combination of times mentioned earlier can be used for practice, either a few bars of each

or using a blues structure as 'Song Three' written earlier (p. 135) or 'Down Another Road'

Tape track 15 has the rhythm section on 'Down Another Road'.

Mood improvising

This is improvising where there are no pre-composed structures. It can be done in two ways:

1. by setting up a subject (ghosts, streams etc.);
2. by the musicians following each other, creating from the ideas set up by each other.

Often such improvising, because of its lack of pulse may sound similar to straight improvising.

Illustrations Record track 15 has the band improvising on the subject of ghosts and *track 16* has them freely improvising with no pre-composed structure.

Spontaneous arranging

Where there is a pre-composed structure it can often be treated in a fresh way at each performance. Some possibilities were mentioned in the section on arranging but further ideas would be:

Free choice of soloist. Unless there is a definite reason for a soloist to be used, the choice should be left till the performance. Occasionally no one will step forward immediately but generally there will be no problem.

Rhythm section decisions should be left to the musicians themselves. Decisions as to resting, playing louder or softer, etc.

Textural decisions can sometimes be left to the band also. A passage like

given to each of the musicians can yield many permutations of texture, by their choice which part they will play.

Overall construction. In some instances a complete composition of smaller pieces can be constructed in this way by using the above ideas with solo cadenzas where the soloist hints at the passage he wishes to go to and the other musicians follow. For example in an extract from *An Odyssey* entitled 'Mr Foggs' the soloist has to hint at one of the three suggested pieces and thus indicate to the other members of the band which piece will follow.

Illustrations Record track 17 has a soloist showing, by indications during his improvised cadenzas, which of the options he is choosing. In the first example he clearly indicates the 6/8 tempo of option one. In the second example he quotes from the melody of option two.

Appendix I   Chords

Complete listing of three and four note chords built on root C

Major type chords (1, 3, 5, 6 or 7 from major scale on root)

(Major, M, Perfect and △ are used to designate a major 7th chord.)

Minor type chords (1, lowered 3rd, 5 and 6 or 7)

(Minor, m or − are used to designate the minor chord.)

Dominant type chords (1, 3, 5, lowered 7)

(The 5th may be raised without altering the nature of the chord.)

Minor 7th type chords (1, lowered 3rd, 5, lowered 7)

(The 5th may be lowered without altering the nature of the chord. Such a chord is sometimes known as a 'half-diminished'.)

Diminished type chords (1, lowered 3, lowered 5 and doubly lowered 7, which is the same as ♮ 6)

(The diminished 7th chord is sometimes wrongly called a diminished 6th.)

There are various systems in use. I have tried to give the commonest ones above. Whatever system you decide to use, stick to it and always write clearly.

Appendix II Chord progressions

The commonest root movements between the chords of conventional chord progressions is up a 5th or down a 4th.

Next strongest are movements up or down a major or minor 2nd, which seem to occur equally over the bar line or within the bar.

Movements of a major or minor 3rd are considered to be weak because many of the notes will be the same usually, so they are most often seen within the bar.

Changes of chord type on the same root are generally seen within the bar also.

e.g. | C   A7 | D−7 G7 | C   C7 | F   F− |
        weak strong   strong   strong   strong
                    strong*   weak   weak

        | E−7 Eb° | D−7 G7 | C   Bb7 | C   ‖
          strong   strong*   strong
                    strong   strong   strong

*The D−7 G7 progression is often seen *within* the bar. The strong root movement is somewhat weakened because there are so many notes in common between the two chords.

(NB Comments regarding the strengths and weaknesses of root movements are relative. Strong root progressions can be constructed from movements of 3rds.)

Most chord progressions in jazz consist of diatonic chords linked by various passing chords, e.g. 'I Got Rhythm' (bars 1 to 8)

```
| Bb    G−7  | C−7   F7  | Bb    G−7  | C−7   F7  |
diatonic ..................................
```

```
| Bb    Bb7 | Eb     Eb−| Bb    F7  | Bb          ||
dia.  passing dia.  passing diatonic .............
```

A correct understanding of the relationships between the chords in such a progression is of great value to the improviser, the accompanying players such as bass, piano and guitar, the arranger and the prospective composer. The improviser and the accompanying players need to know the function of each chord and to know which chords can be substituted for the originals and the effect of such substitutions. They must also recognise any modulations and be able to tell whether they are temporary or permanent. For the arranger the use of substitute chords is a necessary part of his craft. For the composer an understanding of other people's chord progressions is very useful when he comes to write his own.

To simplify the analysis of chord progressions a system has been evolved of roman numerals and chord names. This is particularly helpful when dealing with transposing instruments or when transposing a tune to a new key. The roman numeral patterns – and the sound of the patterns – stays the same and will be more easily recognised.

For example the diatonic chords in a key would be analysed as follows:

```
C Maj 7   D−7    E−7    F Maj 7   G7   A−7    B−7(b5)
I Maj 7   II−7   III−7  IV Maj 7  V7   VI−7   VII−7(b5)
```

The passing chords used are named according to their relationship with the prevailing tonality and can be put into three main groups:

Secondary dominants

The related dominants (7th chords a 5th above) to each of the diatonic chords. In C these would be:
C7(I7) resolving (generally) to F
D7(II7) resolving (generally) to G7
E7 (III7) resolving (generally) to A − 7
F#7(#IV7 not IV#7) resolving (generally) to B − 7(b5)
(G7 is of course the primary dominant)
A7(VI7) resolving (generally) to D − 7
B7(VII7) resolving (generally) to E − 7

These secondary dominants can, as in the bridge of 'I Got Rhythm', form a chain of dominants resolving down a 5th and finally resolving on to a diatonic chord.

```
|| D7  | D7  | G7  | G7  | C7  | C7  | F7  | F7  || (Bb)
   III7        VI7        II7        V7        (I)
```

Secondary supertonics

The related supertonic chords of the secondary dominants. (That is a minor 7th chord a perfect 5th above each secondary dominant, thus bearing the same relationship to the secondary dominants as the supertonic (II−7) bears to the dominant (V7).) As will be seen there is some overlap and these chords may be regarded as having a dual function.

In C these chords would be:

C♯−7(♭5)(♯I−7) resolving, generally to F♯7 (secondary dominant of B−7♭5)
D−7 is the supertonic
E−7(III−7) resolving, generally, to A7 (secondary dominant of D−7)

F♯−7(♭5)(♯IV−7♭5)	,,	B7	,,	E−7
G−7	(V−7)	,,	C7	,,	F
A−7	(VI−7)	,,	D7	,,	G7
B−7♭5	(VII−7♭5)	,,	E7	,,	A−7

Miscellaneous chords

The common miscellaneous chords are

C♯°	♯I°	All diminished chords should be inverted till they
E♭°	♭III°	have ♯I or ♭III as root (II° are rarely used).
F−	IV−	generally used after IV and before I or III−7
D♭7	♭II7	generally resolves to I
D♭ Maj 7	♭II Maj 7	generally resolves to I
A♭7	♭VI7	generally resolves to V7 or ♭II7
A♭ Maj 7	♭VI Maj 7	generally resolves to ♭II Maj 7
B♭ Maj 7	♭VII Maj 7	generally used after IV or before I or VI−7.

This may look complex but there are only twenty-five different chords commonly seen in a diatonically based progression out of a possible fifty-five (eleven chromatic notes and five main chord types). The following analyses should make things clear.

'I Got Rhythm'
Bars 1 to 8

| Bb | G−7 | C−7 | F7 | Bb | G−7 | C−7 | F7 | |
| I | VI−7 | II−7 | V7 | | | | | |

| Bb | Bb7 | Eb | | Eb− | Bb | F7 | Bb | ‖ |
| I | I7 | IV | | IV− | I | V7 | I | |

The progression
used earlier

‖ C   A−7 | D−7   G7 | C   C7 | F   F− |
I   VI−7   II−7   V7   I   I7   IV   IV−

| E−7   Eb° | D−7   G7 | C   Bb7 | C   ‖
III−7   ♭III°   II−7   V7   I   ♭VII7   I

Common patterns

A close look at the preceding examples and other popular song chord progressions will show several recurring patterns, the most obvious being the closing cadence of II−7 V7 I.

Other common patterns are as follows but note these are basic chords. Sometimes different chords are substituted.

(a) I   VI−7 | II−7   V7   found in 'I Got Rhythm', 'Blue Moon', 'What is there to say', 'These Foolish Things', 'The Way You Look To-night' (1 bar per chord).

NB These are basic chords. Sometimes different chords are substituted.

(b) I   ♯I° | II−7   V7   found in 'Deep Purple', 'S'Wonderful', 'Imagination', 'Have You Met Miss Jones' etc.

(c) I   ♭III° | II−7   V7   found in 'The Song is You' (1 bar per chord), 'Penthouse Serenade', 'Blue Room'.

(d) I   I7 | IV   IV−   found in 'The Talk of the Town', 'If I had You', 'Misty', 'I May be Wrong' etc.

(e) II−7 V7 | I   found in 'Body and Soul', 'I'll Never Smile
(as a starting progression)   Again', 'Mad about the Boy' etc.

(f) I   VI7 | II7   V7   found in 'Don't Get Around Much Any
(a variation of (a))   More', 'Darktown Strutters Ball' etc.

(g) IV   IV− | I   found in 'Moonglow', 'After You've Gone',
(as a starting progression)   'Stardust', the bridge of 'Don't Get Around Much Any More'.

Modulations

Not all popular songs stay in one key. Many modulate at the bridge, as was mentioned earlier; others may modulate *within* a section. Often in these instances one or two of the chords may have a dual function (a different role in each key) and a correct analysis will show this.

Be careful that temporary modulations are not confused with movements within the tonality. C C7 | F F− is a common progression in C, but the progression C C7 | F D−7 | G−7 C7 | in C would be a temporary modulation into F. A correct analysis would be

    Pivot chords
C: I   I7 | IV | |
F: V7 | I   VI−7 | II−7   V7 |

'What's New' goes through three keys in the first 8 bars:

(C7)　F　| E♭−7 A♭7 |　　D♭ | G−7(♭5)　C7 |
　　　F−　| G−7(♭5)C7 | F | F ‖ (Basic chords)

It must be remembered that not all chord progressions will easily fit into the patterns mentioned or be analysable in terms of diatonic chords and the various groups of passing chords. These may have been constructed using a different system, such as modal progressions – or in fact no system at all. Some of the possibilities are mentioned later but such 'rules' as have been already given are simply guidelines to establish a general policy and are not meant to cover every possibility.

Correcting chord progressions

The following example shows some of the common faults and how they should be corrected.

C　　E°　|　D−7　G♭°　|　A7　　　|　D−　　G7　|
better as
C　　C♯°　|　D−7　E♭°　|　E−7　A7　|　D−7　G7　|

| Diminished chords should be inverted to become ♯I° or ♭III°. This gives a better root progression. | Secondary supertonics can be added. | II− chords should usually be changed to II−7. |

| C　A−7 | F　　G7 | C C6 C Maj 7 | C6 C Maj 9 C Maj 7 |
better as
| C　A−7 | D−7　G7 | C (or possibly C Maj 7)　　　　‖

IV to V7 is better as II−7 to V7. (IV− V7 is better as II−7(♭5) to V7.)

Take away all extra chords unless necessary. E.g. the progression D− D−⁺5 | D−6 D−7 | shows a strong line between the chords and all the alterations need to be marked.

The patterns mentioned earlier can often be used when trying to correct wrong chords.

Appendix III   Substitute chords

Many chord progressions can be improved by the use of substitute chords, but they should not be used indiscriminately and should always fit the melody. They are derived by changing the notes of a chord around (A−7 for C) or by using a strong root progression with a slightly altered upper structure. Their main uses are:

to strengthen a weak root progression

to create tension

to create surprise.

Some common substitutes are:

1. III−7 in place of I

Here the substitute strengthens the root progression and creates more tension.

2. VI−7 in place of I

Here the substitute strengthens the root progression.

3. ♭II7 in place of V7 (its best use would be to control the degree of tension)

Note the two strongest notes of the chord – the 3rd and the 7th – are common to both chords

D♭7 best here as ♯11 resolves correctly

148

G7 best as ♭9 tension resolves correctly, but both could be used.

Either G7 gives 9 to ♭9 – strong but good,

 D♭7 gives ♭13 to ♭5 – less strong, still good.

 4. ♭VII7 in place of IV−. Note that ♭VII7 always resolves to I and is not the dominant *of* anything, as for example, C7 is the dominant of F in the key of C.

The root progression is strengthened and more tension created.

 5. For sustained tonic

 I II−7 III−7 II−7 if it continues with I

 I II−7 III−7 ♭III° if it goes to II−7

 6. For diminished chords:

 For ♯I° use a V7(♭9), a major 3rd beneath the root, with its preceding II−7(♭5)

 For ♭III° use a V7(♭9) a major 3rd beneath the root with its preceding II−7(♭5)

These substitutions are used even if the resolution seems wrong, as in the following, exaggerated, example

7. For a sustained minor chord

 I− I− Maj 7 I−7 I−6

8. For a long II—7   V7
use II—(triad) II—(Maj 7) II—7 V7

Turnarounds

Various progressions can be used to fill in at the end of an 8-bar phrase where
the tonic is normally sustained for 2 bars. Some of the patterns mentioned
earlier are useful and substitute chords such as ♭II7 for V7 can also be used.

I	VI—7	II—7	V7
I	♯I°	II—7	V7
I	♭III°	II—7	V7
I	VI7	II7	V7

Also possible, but to be used with care, are variations of

	I	♭III	♭VI	♭II	
	I	♭III	♭VI	♭II	
in C	C	E♭	A♭	D♭	
giving	C	E♭7	A♭7	D♭7	
or	C	E♭7	A♭ Maj 7	D♭7	
	C	E♭ Maj 7	A♭ Maj 7	D♭ Maj 7	etc.

Substitute chords in place of the initial tonic would give possibilities like

	(V7)	VI—7	II7	II—7	V7
in C	(G7)	A—7	D7	D—7	G7
or	(V7)	III—7	VI7	II—7	V7
	(G7)	E—7	A7	D—7	G7
or	(V7)	III—7	♭III7	♭VI Maj 7	♭II Maj 7
	(G7)	E—7	E♭7	A♭ Maj 7	D♭ Maj 7

Appendix IV   Alterations and extensions to chords

Major type chords

9 can be used on major 7 and 6 chords.
11, which must be raised and supported by 9, is sometimes used.
13 is sometimes used (supported by 9 and sometimes by ♯11).

Minor type chords

9 is used on minor type chords (with 6th or major 7th).
13 is sometimes used.

Dominant type chords

9 can be natural, lowered or raised.

11 can be raised or natural.
   If ♮11 is used, the 3rd is often omitted to avoid a ♭9 interval.
   ♭9 is usually used for support.

13 can be natural or lowered.
   If lowered 13 is used, the 5th is either omitted or lowered, to avoid the ♭9 interval.

♮9 is used to support ♮13.

Lowered 9 is used to support lowered 13.

Raised 11 may be used to support 13 but is not necessary.

5 can be altered by being lowered, possibly to support ♭13, or raised, when it becomes an augmented chord.

Minor 7th type chords

9 is natural on −7 chords but is lowered if used on −7(♭5) chords.

11 is natural and supported by the relevant 9th.

13 is not used.

Diminished type chords

9 is natural.

11 is natural.

13 is lowered.

Major 7th may be used.

This can result in what is known as a double-diminished chord.

Appendix V   The rhythm section

The rhythm section in jazz usually consists of piano or guitar, in some cases both, providing the chords, bass providing the basis pulse and suggesting the harmony, and drums providing and decorating the pulse.

The piano (or guitar) provides the harmonic structure. This is done by what is known as comping (complementing) – playing the basic structure in a rhythmic way to assist the soloist. At first it may be desirable to play sustained chords. Try to spread these out, and avoid duplicating the bass. For a simple C− figure

possible voicings would be

and possible rhythms

This approach can be tried with the basic blues progressions.
Possible voicings for the dominant 7th blues sequence would be

The bass should suggest the harmonic structure and provide the pulse – which would normally involve playing in 4 beats to the bar.

A possible line for the blues sequence would be

The joining between the chord notes can be either from the scale or chromatic.

The drums consists of several instruments:
   The bass drum which provides either a very light basic pulse

or rhythmic accents such as

The hi-hat (two cymbals operated by a foot pedal) which provides an offbeat

Other rhythms more normally played on the cymbal can also be played – with sticks – on the hi-hat.

The cymbal which provides the basic time

The snare drum which adds accents and fills. For slow tempos brushes may be used on the snare to provide the basic beat, sometimes known as 'stirring soup'.

The successful combination of all these functions is a major problem for most beginning drummers. At first they must try to be as simple as possible. The basic pulse is what matters – not what fancy decorations can be added to it.

Over and above their individual roles the rhythm section must act as a team, working with each other and reacting to ideas (dynamics, accents etc.) thrown up within the rhythm section and by the soloist. A lot can be learnt from listening to records.

On long passages of one chord – or scalic pieces – piano voicings and bass lines should be made interesting with other diatonic voicings from the mode on the lines of

REFERENCES

Listening

Listen to the tape of the rhythm section and the Illustrations Record. The Lecture Concert Record contains some remixed passages to make the rhythm section more prominent. Good rhythm section tracks on the *Anthology* are:

'I've got you under my skin' – J. J. Johnson (fairly conventional).

'As Catch Can' – Gerry Mulligan (pianoless rhythm section).

'Sweet Sue' – Miles Davis (good rhythm section).

'Waltz Limps' – Dave Brubeck (rhythm in 3/4).

'Two Bass Hit' – John Coltrane and Miles Davis (over-recorded drums but good).

'Chappaqua Suite' – Ornette Coleman (pianoless rhythm section, very modern).

Also listen to the rhythm sections of the Miles Davis band of the late fifties (Paul Chambers bass, Red Garland or Wynton Kelly piano, and Philly Joe Jones drums) or the band of the mid-sixties (Ron Carter bass, Herbie Hancock piano, and Tony Williams drums). Also the John Coltrane group of the sixties (Jimmy Garrison bass, McCoy Tyner piano, and Elvin Jones drums.)

Reading

Jazz Improvisation by John Mehegan (Watson–Guptill Publications, New York). Mostly concerned with piano.

Improvising Jazz by Jerry Coker (Prentice Hall Inc. paperback).

Ray Brown Bass Method by Ray Brown (Ray Brown Music, 1963).

How To Play Blues Piano by Junior Mance (Ray Brown Music).

Jazz Exercises and Pieces by Oscar Peterson (Ray Brown Music).

Buddy Rich's Modern Interpretations of Snare Drum Rudiments by Buddy Rich (Embassy Music, 1942).

Advanced Techniques for the Modern Drummer by Jim Chapin (Jim Chapin, 1964).

Appendix VI Ranges and transpositions

(The ranges are given in concert.)

Trumpet

Transposes up a tone.
  The flugelhorn is the same but the upper range is more limited.

Trombone

Non-transposing.

Saxophones

All saxophones are written in treble clef.

Soprano   Alto   Tenor   Baritone

Soprano transposes up a tone.
Alto transposes up a major 6th.
Tenor transposes up a tone and an octave.
Baritone transposes up a major 6th and an octave.

Clarinet

Usually in B♭.

Transposes up a tone.

Bass clarinet

Written in treble clef.

Transposes up a tone and an octave.

Flute

Non-transposing.

Alto flute

Transposes up a 4th.

Guitar

Transposes up an octave.

Vibes

String bass

Transposes up an octave. Note that if a *real* unison is desired with the piano the piano must be written down an octave from the written bass notes.

The bass guitar transposes the same as the string bass.

The Lecture Concert Record demonstrates the range and extremes of range of most of the common jazz instruments.

Appendix VII Modes and scales

The scales used on the common chord types can be classified as follows (all examples are on root C):

Major type

As I of C

As IV of G

Minor type

As I of C—

Can be melodic or harmonic scale or combination.

Dominant type

As V7 of F

as ♭VII7 of D

All alterations should be shown in the scale, but a good scale for use with most alterations would be

160

The whole-tone scale is also useful, particularly for ♭5 and ♯5

Minor 7th chords

As II −7 in B♭

As III −7 in A♭

As VI −7 in E♭

As VII −7(♭5) in D♭

Diminished chords

Because of their tonal ambiguity a special diminished scale is used

This scale can also be used for −7 chords, −7(♭5) chords, major 7th chords, −6 chords and on a dominant chord a semitone beneath (i.e. on a B7 in this case).

Another possible scale is the 'blues scale' which can be used throughout a blues sequence.

Five-note scales such as pentatonic, Hirayoshi etc. can be effectively used.

Many of the above scales conform to the modes constructed from the diatonic notes of a key. They are shown below constructed on root C.

The commonest mode used in jazz is the Dorian, with the Phrygian, Aeolian and Lydian also being used.

Appendix VIII Transformation techniques

The following are some of the simpler transformation techniques. It must be remembered that these are mechanical devices that need to be combined and used with much musical thought before they can be effective.

All transpositions use

as the basic motif.

Melodic transformations

1. Literal transposition, changing the level of the pitch exactly.

2. Tonal transposition, conforming to a specific scale – in this case C.

3. Contour transposition, keeping the general shape but not exactly.

Rhythmic transformations

1. Regular augmentation, increasing the value of each note in the same ratio.

2. Regular diminution, decreasing the value of each note in the same ratio.

3. Irregular augmentation.

4. Irregular diminution.

5. Displacement, changing the starting note of the motif.

6. Change of time signature.

7. Use of the rhythm only.

Other transformations

1. Inversion, which can be literal,

tonal,

or by contour.

2. Retrograde, starting at the back and working forward. This is best when combined with a change of rhythm.

3. Adding notes at the beginning, the end or the inside.

4. Subtracting notes.

Other possibilities are new harmonisation, new orchestration and the interchange of motifs within a piece, and combinations of the above.

REFERENCES

The Thematic Process In Music by Rudolph Reti (Faber, 1961).

Glossary

Some words and expressions which may be unfamiliar, especially in their jazz context, are explained in this short glossary.

avant garde   Applied in jazz since the late 1950s to the more extreme groups, particularly those who play without a recurring pulse.

bebop, bop   Onomatopoeic expression of the sounds used in jazz of the early 1940s typified by the intense music of such as Charlie Parker and Dizzie Gillespie.

blowing group   A group that often doesn't bother with pre-written arrangements but uses tunes that all know.

cool   Term used for the jazz played on the West Coast of America in the early 1950s, since applied to any soft introverted sounds.

cycle of 5ths   An extension of the dominant–tonic progression to include all the notes of the chromatic scale: C/F/Bb/Eb/Ab etc.

fill   A short improvised section, possibly between two written parts or behind a written melody.

funky   Literally dirty music, with a blues feel and notes and instrumental tones distorted.

head arrangement   Arrangement made up in performance most often on a repeated form like the blues with the musicians improvising *riffs*.

hi-hat   Two cymbals operated by a system of rods and a foot pedal, the cymbal on top lifting and falling on the lower one.

mode   Scales distinguished from diatonic scales and each other by their special arrangement of tones and semitones, e.g. the Dorian mode, the most commonly used mode in jazz, can be represented on the piano by the white notes starting at D and has the pattern tone/semitone/tone/tone/tone/semitone/tone.

rhythm   Often used loosely to describe the regular recurring beat or pulse.

riff   Repeated rhythmically based motifs or patterns, often used in the music of the swing era, the bands building them up section by section.

rock   From rock and roll, used most often to refer to an 8 beats in the bar feel.

scat singing   Nonsense syllables in the style of an instrumental improvisation.

straight   Used in place of terms such as classical, serious, European etc. It is less inaccurate and contrasts with the musical freeness of jazz.

swing era   The period during the 1930s when the big bands were *the* popular

166

music of the day. The most famous band was Benny Goodman's and he was known as the King of Swing.

tom-toms Drums between bass drum and snare drum in tone and size; the larger ones are placed on the floor, the smaller ones mounted on the bass drum.

trad Dixieland or New Orleans style.

vibraphone, vibes Instrument similar to xylophone but with metal keys. The sound is amplified by resonating tubes and the characteristic vibrato effect is created by revolving discs fitted over the tubes.

voicing The choice and placing of notes in a chord and the choice of instruments to play them.

wah wah Pedal-operated device used to alter the sound of instruments electronically. Most often used on the guitar. Makes a sound rather like a baby crying.